Hacked!

Dr Gareth Moore B.Sc (Hons) M.Phil Ph.D is the internationally best-selling author of a wide range of brain-training and puzzle books for both children and adults, including *Enigma: Crack the Code*, *Ultimate Dot to Dot*, *Brain Games for Clever Kids*, *Lateral Logic* and *Extreme Mazes*. His books have sold millions of copies in the UK alone, and have been published in over thirty different languages. He is also the creator of online brain-training site BrainedUp.com, and runs the daily puzzle site PuzzleMix.com.

Web: DrGarethMoore.com
Twitter: @DrGarethMoore
YouTube: YouTube.com/@DrGareth

Laura Jayne Ayres is a puzzle writer and researcher. After studying Linguistics at the University of Cambridge, she worked as a playwright before joining Dr Gareth Moore's puzzle team. Books that she has worked on include *The Great British Puzzle Book*, *The Perfect Crime Puzzle Book*, *The Nautical Puzzle Book* and *The Ordnance Survey Kids' Adventure Book*.

Hacked!

The Cyber Crime Puzzle Book

DR GARETH MOORE
LAURA JAYNE AYRES

Michael O'Mara Books Limited

First published in Great Britain in 2023 by
Michael O'Mara Books Limited
9 Lion Yard
Tremadoc Road
London SW4 7NQ

A CIP catalogue record for this book is available from the British Library.

Papers used by Michael O'Mara Books Limited are natural, recyclable products made from wood grown in sustainable forests. The manufacturing processes conform to the environmental regulations of the country of origin.

ISBN: 978-1-78929-472-9 in paperback print format

1 2 3 4 5 6 7 8 9 10

Designed and typeset by Gareth Moore
Includes images from Adobe Stock and from Shutterstock.com

Printed and bound by CPI Group (UK) Ltd, Croydon, CR0 4YY

www.mombooks.com

FSC
www.fsc.org

MIX
Paper | Supporting
responsible forestry
FSC® C171272

Contents

Introduction

Welcome to *Hacked!: The Cyber Crime Puzzle Book*. Within these pages, you'll find plenty of puzzles to challenge your inner computer whizz-kid. Whether you're a helpless victim or a tactical mastermind, however, is up to you.

Not all hackers are bad guys, so in this book you'll find that you're variously both the target *and* agent of some unusual online activity. Each puzzle is presented on either a single page or a pair of two facing pages, with a large title and puzzle number to help you keep track. Whatever the situation you're presented with in the explanatory text, each puzzle will finish with a prompt question to be directly answered – so that's a good place to start if you're not sure what's being asked of you. The **part in bold** is the most important section.

It's important to note that you won't need any real-world knowledge, or even any technology, to solve the puzzles in this book. There are no trick questions, so all the information you might need to crack any particular conundrum will be given to you on the page already. The puzzles are designed to be solved offline, so all you'll require is a sharp pencil and an equally sharp mind to make your way through.

Numbered solutions can be found at the back of the book for you to check your answers, or in some cases see what reasoning could have helped you find that answer. Most of the solutions are in the form of a numerical code or short phrase, but it should always be clear from each individual puzzle what's expected. For visual puzzles, the solution image will be given in full so that you can check it against your own result, if you wish – but therefore be careful when checking other answers, since you could be easily 'spoiled' by glimpsing part of another solution. If that does happen, skip that puzzle for now and come back to it later when the memory will hopefully have faded.

Equally, if you find yourself stuck on a puzzle, you can use the solutions at the back to give you a hint. The best way to do this is to get a trusty friend to read the explanation for you and see if they can give you an extra clue, but if you're solving on your own then try using a piece of paper to slowly reveal more of the answer. Or if you're really bamboozled by a puzzle, move onto the next one and come back to it later. And, of course, if you're really not enjoying a puzzle for any reason, then just skip to another one – the idea is to have fun while hacking, after all!

It goes without saying – but I will say it anyway – that all of the situations in the book are entirely fictional, and any similarity with the real world is just pure chance. It's not intentional.

Although there is some natural variation in the difficulty level of the various puzzles, remember that all of them are intended to be actually solved so there is always *some* way to make progress. Equally, they are not arranged in any particular story order, so you are welcome to start solving the puzzles from any page that you like. If, for example, you prefer picture-based puzzles then you might find that flicking through the book and choosing the most eye-catching puzzle is a good way so start. Or you might want to start at the very beginning. There's no wrong way to get going, no right way to solve, and no time like the present to do so.

Happy solving!

Dr Gareth Moore

1. Logging In

You open your email and see that you've received an encoded image. Ah, this could be the log-in PIN you've been waiting for. You'd better decode it and find out!

To reveal what is hidden inside the image, shade some squares according to the clue numbers. These clues provide, in reading order from left to right or top to bottom, the length of every run of consecutive shaded squares in each row and column. There must be a gap of at least one empty square between each run of shaded squares in the same row or column.

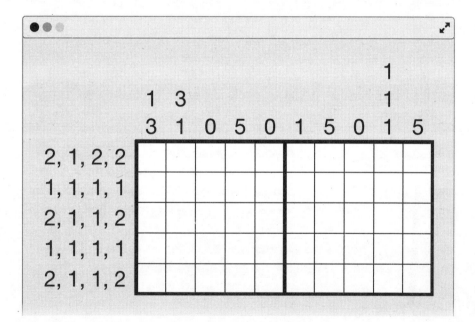

Is it the PIN? If so, what digits does it consist of?

2. Odd and Even

You're waiting on an old friend to send you a password that should unlock some encrypted files. Your phone beeps – you've received a text message. Wait, make that two text messages. You know that combining the messages somehow will give you the password you need.

Can you work out what the password is?

4826
KTAU

95713
SRPBN

3. Binary Problem

You're working with some old-school software, and need to brush up on your binary. You're looking for a passcode that you need to unlock the next stage of a program, and apparently the solution can be found in the grid below.

Place a '0' or '1' into every empty square so that there are an equal number of each digit in every row and column. Reading along a row or column, there may be no more than two of the same digit in succession. When complete, the penultimate row will be the passcode you need, reading from left to right. **What is it?**

	0		1			1	1
1	0		1				
		1				0	
		0			1	1	
	1	1			1		
	0				0		
				0		0	0
0	1			1		0	

4. Funny Turn

An email drops into your inbox with a link you've been waiting for. You're expecting a 6-digit temporary username for a new secret account you've set up – but when you open it up, all you see is this:

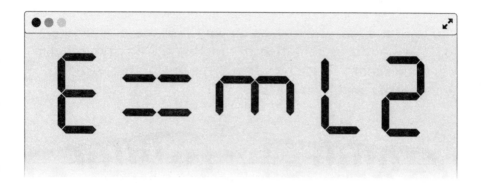

At the bottom of the email, you see the sender has included some symbols in their signature:

These must be a clue. **What, then, is your username?**

5. The Counterfeit Chips

A bunch of chips have just been delivered which you are planning to use to upgrade each of your systems, but the moment you pull them out of their electrostatically protective bag your keen eye spots something that doesn't seem quite right.

You lay out a few of the chips on your work desk, and take a look. Aha – there's something wrong here! One of these chips has been slightly modified when compared to the rest. **Can you identify which one it is?**

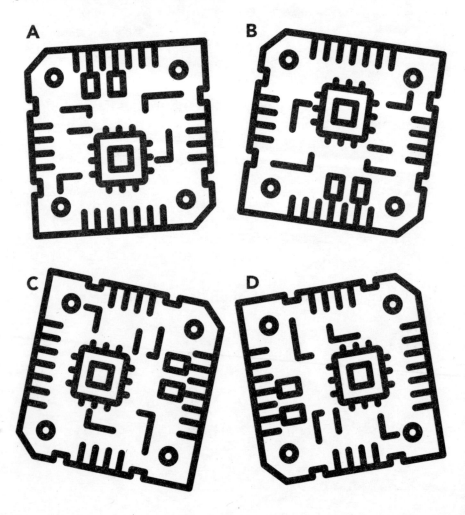

6. Corrupted Transmission

A strange email arrives, which is par for the course – and you know better than to simply open it and hope for the best. Instead, you quarantine it and start up a clean virtual machine, carefully configured so it has no access to the outside world.

You open the email, and discover the intriguing screen below. It seems that someone is trying to send you a message, but every other line appears to be corrupt. **Can you decode it?**

```
transmission initiated...
Γ  ¿  º Δ× Ω  ¥  ± Φ¿×º

download begun... 100% complete
¥± Φ  Δ Δ × ¿ º ± Φ ¥ Ω Γ Ω

opening data packet... decrypting...
Γ Ω ¥ Δ Ω ¥Γ ¿ ± Φ × Δ Γ  º

file has been extracted
± Φ Ω ¥ ΓΓΩΓ ¿¥ºΩ Ω ¥

format identified: text/plain
Γ ¿ ºΩ ¥×Γ ± Φ × Δ ¥ Ω ¥

spooling contents to output
Φ ¿ º Ω ¥× ±  × ΓΔ¿ º

THE DAY HAS COME
¥Ω  ±Γ Φ¿ º Δ ¥Ω×

I AM YOUR OMEGA
Γ  ¿Δ º± ×Φ Ω  ¥

PAY ATTENTION TO ONLY MY SYMBOL
Γ  ± Φ  Δ Ω Ω¥ ¥  Γ Γ¿ º  ×
```

7. The Strange Printout

An odd piece of paper drops through your real-world letterbox, full of geometric shapes. **What does it say?**

READ THE SIXTH LETTER OF

EACH SEPARATE LINE

I HAVE LISTED HERE

AND I SPELL OUT THE MESSAGE

I WISH MOSTLY TO COMMUNICATE

TO YOU EXTREMELY URGENTLY

8. The Digital Clock

There's something wrong with your digital clock, which is a problem because it contains a special circuit that you use for extracting time-sensitive encryption keys.

You take a look at the circuit with your multimeter, and measure the digital state that is being sent to each segment of the LED display.

In a digital circuit, a '0' represents an 'off' state while a '1' represents an 'on' state. **What time should the clock be displaying at the moment**, given the measurements below?

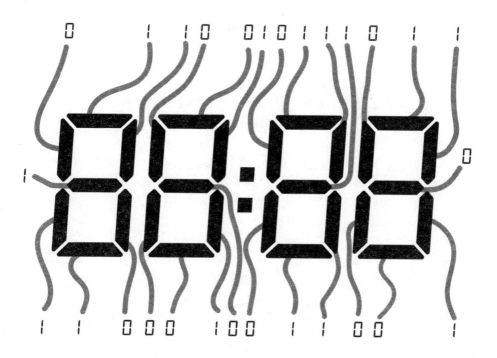

9. Secret Signals

You've been communicating with someone online who wants you to take them on as a client. You have an encrypted chat session going on, but you're especially wary at the moment because some of your recent work has been only semi-legal, and you don't want to get caught out.

This potential client wants you to hack into the computer of someone particularly high-profile, so you decide you need to meet the client first. It wouldn't be the first time someone's tried to catch you out by pretending to have a big scoop to uncover, only to turn out to have been working for the other side all along.

You've asked them for a few personal details, and their replies have been worryingly vague. So you send the following message in the chat:

> I need to verify you. What's your phone number?

This is a great test of trust. Once someone has given you their phone number they know they're easier to track, so those with bad intent won't be keen to reveal it.

You wait a while and there's no response. Perhaps you've scared them off, fearing that you could find their location and identify them from this information?

But eventually they do send a reply:

> Don't take it personally but I don't trust anyone, so I can't share in plain text. Someone has been tracking me.
>
> My phone 'number' is: +DFIBHEGAIC

You stare at the message. What is this?! You start to wonder if they are simply trolling you – and what other information they might have on you already.

You message them back to tell them you don't understand what they've sent over, and they soon reply:

> That's fair enough – I don't expect you to trust me any more than I trust you. So here's another few pieces of information – perhaps you can figure it all out and identify me a little better.
>
> My 'name' is 3814.

Once again they seem not to have given you a straight answer, and you feel more than a little frustrated.

When you look more closely at the two messages, however, you realize they've actually given you all the information you need to verify them after all.

What is their phone number, and what is their first name?

10. Keep Your Friends Close

There are a few hackers you know by name – or at least, the alias they use the most. You wouldn't necessarily call them friends, but piece by piece you've been able to work out a little more about their lives. It's always helpful to know something about who your 'colleagues' really are, whatever your line of work.

Over the past few years, you've collected information about three people in particular: Jack, Hopper and Marco. They all have different 'civilian' jobs on the side, and live in different cities around the world.

You're about to take a trip to Sydney, and want to meet up with the person who lives there. **Who is it, and what is their civilian job?**

You should be able to work it from the following notes:

- Marco isn't the police officer

- Hopper works as an accountant

- The person living in Paris is not the engineer

- Marco isn't the one living in London

11. Find the Pattern

Some people are more safety-conscious than others, and every now and again you come across a regular computer user that actually does what most security experts recommend: change their passwords frequently.

You've been doing your best to keep tabs on a particular target, but they keep switching their passwords every month – which is good for them, but bad for you. You're ready for the switch each time, but still... it's annoying to be made to work harder for the information.

You're still able to work out what their passwords are each month, so ultimately it's all just wasted effort for them. You write down their passwords as you go, keeping a careful record. When you look closely at the notes you've taken, however, it doesn't look totally random. Here are the last few months' passwords, which each consists of multiple numbers. **Can you work out what the next password will be, to replace the question marks below?**

999-990-981-972

888-870-852-834

777-750-723-696

666-630-594-558

555-510-465-420

???-???-???-???

12. Building Blocks

Not every day is a 'school day' – sometimes it's nice to kick back and play a few computer games, just like the good old days.

You've been playing around with a world-building game involving cube-like structures, building a little city as you go. The game is pretty simple: to build structures, you can only add or remove cubes to or from pre-existing buildings.

You realize you've added too many cubes to one of your buildings, so you write some code that should remove a few blocks.

The code should work in sequence, removing one block at a time. The result is shown at each stage, to check you're happy with the progress. In the log below, image 1 is the first result, image 2 is the second, and so on:

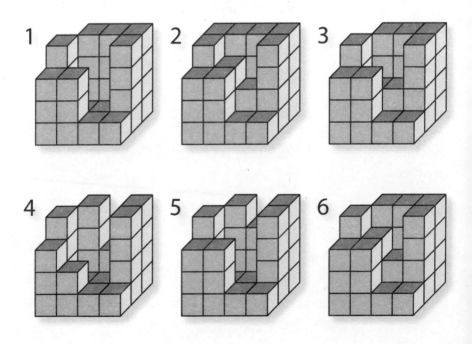

But when you study the results of your code, something doesn't look right. For a start, there are quite a few differences between images 1 and 2. What's going on?

The game is now coming up with an error code:

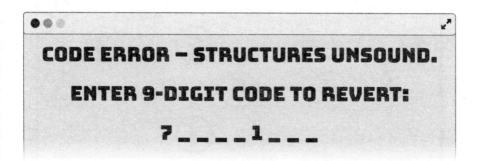

CODE ERROR – STRUCTURES UNSOUND.

ENTER 9-DIGIT CODE TO REVERT:

7 _ _ _ _ 1 _ _ _

Not ideal – you don't want to destroy your city! You had better revert your progress, and undo the errors you made in your code.

What 9-digit code is required, so that you can get your city back on track – and return to the hard job of relaxing?

13. Network Connect

Like any decent hacker, you've got more than one device at your fingertips. To help you keep track of what's hooked up to what, you've drawn yourself a sketch of your various bits of hardware: different processors, screens and so on. On your system map below, each circled number represents a device. **Can you connect them all up to form a network?**

Join devices with horizontal or vertical cables; no more than two cables may join any pair of devices, and no cables may cross. Each device must have as many cables connected to it as specified by its value. The finished layout must connect all devices, so you can follow one or more cables from one device to any other device.

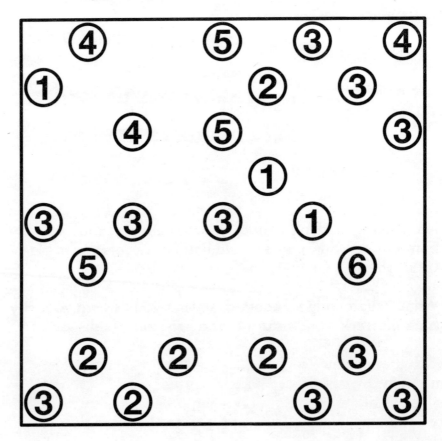

14. Fight or Flight

You've been dipping in and out of air traffic control data from your local airport – it's for a client, and nothing sinister. One day, while idly skimming through the data, you notice some unusual numbers, with certain digits replaced by question marks:

1143 +15 = 0?43

1805 +4 = 2205

0123 -4 = 2123

0?08 -8 = 0008

1111 +11 = ??11

1422 -3 = 1122

2345 +1 = 004?

At first you thought they were a part of certain flight numbers, but now you're not so sure. Although they seem to be linked to journeys that are commencing in your local area, you notice that all of those journeys are long-haul.

With that in mind, can you replace each of the question marks in the data above with its correct digit? Putting all those digits together in reading order, what number results?

15. The Search is On

This is embarrassing... you've forgotten one of your own passcodes! It's a 10-digit number, which means there are 10 billion possible combinations to try. Luckily, you do at least know that none of the digits 0 to 9 repeat within the passcode, so that brings the number of options down to 'just' a few million.

After much trial and error, you've narrowed it down considerably further to only the following possibilities, which you've written on a scrap of paper:

4217359086

3495728061

7148592063

0514762839

6482957130

9426583170

5160834972

8614952730

2631957804

1234567890

You anticipated you might one day forget the number you needed and so you previously designed an unusual retrieval method. **All of the potential codes on your scrap of paper can be found in the grid below, reading in any direction, except for one – the passcode you need. What is it?**

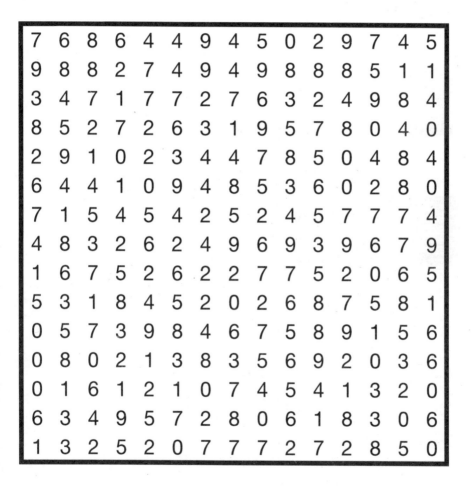

7	6	8	6	4	4	9	4	5	0	2	9	7	4	5
9	8	8	2	7	4	9	4	9	8	8	8	5	1	1
3	4	7	1	7	7	2	7	6	3	2	4	9	8	4
8	5	2	7	2	6	3	1	9	5	7	8	0	4	0
2	9	1	0	2	3	4	4	7	8	5	0	4	8	4
6	4	4	1	0	9	4	8	5	3	6	0	2	8	0
7	1	5	4	5	4	2	5	2	4	5	7	7	7	4
4	8	3	2	6	2	4	9	6	9	3	9	6	7	9
1	6	7	5	2	6	2	2	7	7	5	2	0	6	5
5	3	1	8	4	5	2	0	2	6	8	7	5	8	1
0	5	7	3	9	8	4	6	7	5	8	9	1	5	6
0	8	0	2	1	3	8	3	5	6	9	2	0	3	6
0	1	6	1	2	1	0	7	4	5	4	1	3	2	0
6	3	4	9	5	7	2	8	0	6	1	8	3	0	6
1	3	2	5	2	0	7	7	7	2	7	2	8	5	0

16. Dramatic Downloads

Someone's been trying to hack your machine by exploiting a known bug in receiving emails with attachments which overflow an internal code buffer. The exploit works by making the attachments larger on decoding than they first appear. Nice try, but you know about it – and you're on to them.

Here are the five file sizes as they first appear, with your size-increase calculations added on:

1. **46MB** + *1/3rd of its true size*

2. **265MB** + *3/8th of its true size*

3. **364MB** + *3/7th of its true size*

4. **282MB** + *1/3rd of its true size*

5. **165MB** + *2/3rd of its true size*

Calculate the true size of each file, and work out how many gigabytes the five files unpack to in total.

Note: there are 1,024MB in a gigabyte (GB).

17. Asterisky Business

You've been tasked with unlocking a phone which has been sent to you for one-time access. Even though it's a throwaway device, security is still a priority – the person who sent it to you wants to keep the information that is hidden on the phone away from prying eyes.

In a separate email, the sender tells you that you'll need a 4-digit passcode to unlock the phone, and sends the following image:

None of the five digits in the message seem to form part of the unlock code, and in any case you know you need a 4-digit number to unlock it.

Then your sender pings over another cryptic message:

    Pay attention to ****.

What is the unlock code?

18. Isolation Issues

Disaster! You've clicked on something you shouldn't have, and you've been infected by a nasty virus. That's the last thing you need. So far, your existing files seem to have remained intact, but you can see that the virus has somehow planted one additional file in every folder of your hard drive. Hmmm.

Whoever sent you this malware has also kindly sent you some maintenance notes, to help you contain the spread. After clicking on the dodgy link, the following message popped up:

> Whoops! Gotcha. I've been following your progress for a while now, and I think I could use a friend like you. You and I seem to be on the same page - our work may not always be strictly legal, but at least it is ethical. We are on the right side of history.
>
> Here's a little challenge for you, to see if you have the skills I'm looking for in a partner. This line of work is risky business, and I want to know that you'll be good at damage control. You've probably spotted that there's a little bug sitting in every folder on your hard drive at the moment. Luckily for you, there's a way to contain them before they spread further, and start to eat things.
>
> Imagine that the image below is your hard drive, and each of these dots is a bug you want to contain. Smaller grid squares represent space on the drive, and some of these bugs are more destructive than others - so they need extra room. Draw along the dashed lines to divide the hard-drive grid into squares measuring 1x1 units or larger, with no unused areas left over. Do it so that every square you draw contains exactly one bug.

I want to see how you think. Are you able
to isolate these threats? And, importantly,
can you work well under pressure? I hope so,
because if you get this task wrong, who knows
when the virus will finish deploying? Good
luck - and speak soon, if you succeed.

Why can't you ever just have a quiet day? You're far from sure
that this sender has your best interests at heart, but you scroll
down and take a look at the grid they've sent you:

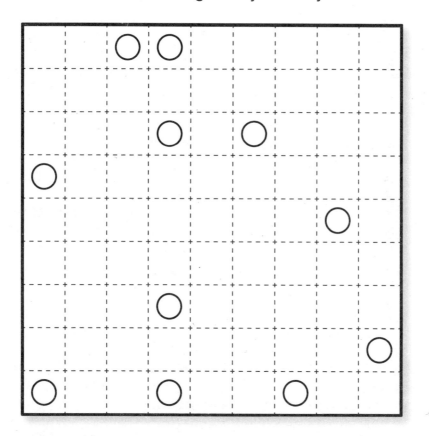

**Can you do as they ask, and isolate the hypothetical viruses
– before a very real one is unleashed on your computer?**

19. Divide and Recover

Someone's broken into your apartment and taken a USB stick. It's good that they didn't take anything else, but you really need the files on that stick to remain for your eyes only. At least the USB stick is fitted with a tracker, giving you an approximate area to search. Unfortunately, however, you only have four hours – after that, the battery will start to die. That's assuming that the person who took it doesn't disable it first, of course.

Here's the rough shape of your search area:

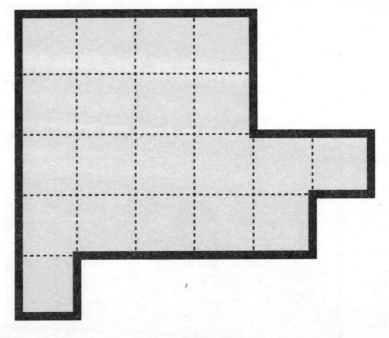

Split up the area into four equal sections to search, so you can spend one hour searching each one. This should hopefully allow you to search in the most efficient way on the ground.

To mark these four sections, draw along some of the dashed grid lines to divide the space into four regions. The regions must all be identical in shape and size, although they may be rotated (but not reflected) relative to one another.

20. No Repeats

You've hidden a 'kill switch' passcode in this grid, which was generated for safekeeping. If anyone tries to compromise your network, inputting this 10-digit number code will shut everything down before access is gained. It's a rarely needed code, so you don't have it memorized – you just know it's the only full row, column or diagonal with no repeated digits.

When you find it, read from top to bottom or left to right to reveal the code. **What's your kill switch?**

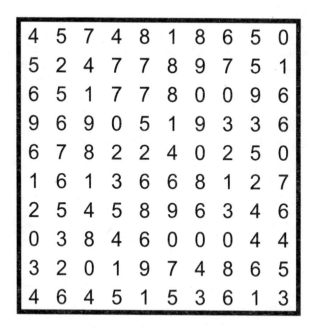

4	5	7	4	8	1	8	6	5	0
5	2	4	7	7	8	9	7	5	1
6	5	1	7	7	8	0	0	9	6
9	6	9	0	5	1	9	3	3	6
6	7	8	2	2	4	0	2	5	0
1	6	1	3	6	6	8	1	2	7
2	5	4	5	8	9	6	3	4	6
0	3	8	4	6	0	0	0	4	4
3	2	0	1	9	7	4	8	6	5
4	6	4	5	1	5	3	6	1	3

21. Threat Levels

You've been trying to remove some malware from your system that you think was sent deliberately by a so-called hacker 'friend' of yours. Just as you think you've got rid of the last of it, the following email drops into your inbox, with an image attached:

Hi there. You've been telling people I'm shady – so here's a shady task for you. Open the attachment and try the following:

- Shade some squares according to the clue numbers I've kindly provided you with.

- These clues provide, in reading order from left to right or top to bottom, the length of every run of consecutive shaded squares in each row and column.

- There must be a gap of at least one empty square between each run of shaded squares in the same row or column.

- When you're done and dusted, take a step back and see what you've created. And let's just say I could press this if you mess with me again.

You open the image, and all you see is the following grid:

It's obviously something they want you to puzzle out for yourself. **What image is revealed by the grid?**

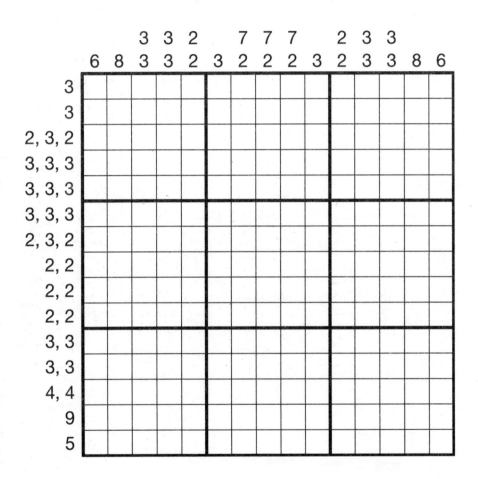

22. Unite and Conquer

You've been communicating with someone high-up in the government – not your usual style, but you believe they are one of the good guys. They've been keeping an extremely low profile – so exposure would be disastrous for both of you – but, finally, they let you in on what they need from you.

By way of an explanation, they've sent you three different emails, one after another. **Can you work out from their cryptic communication what the secret task is?**

● ● ●   Email 1

F N
M
S C E
O L N
F L E

● ● ●   Email 2

I D
Y
E R T
N I E
O D R

● ● ●   Email 3

One thing at a time: 1 then 2 then 1 and so on

23. The Drop

Someone shady has just sent you an access passcode made up of five digits. You're not sure you trust this person, who usually moves in the shadows, and so you think they might be trying to trip you up. Here's the image they sent:

You try entering 68532 but it doesn't work – the digits are correct, but in the wrong order. It looks like the image they sent has been doctored somehow, and you realize you can only have one more attempt.

You really don't want to get this wrong, so what code should you enter?

24. Scanned Entry

A letter drops onto your doormat, apparently delivered by hand. Not ideal – you don't like the idea of people knowing where you live – but you open it anyway. A few pieces of paper drop out, along with a small USB stick. That's pretty odd...

There's a long note in the envelope, and you open it up carefully in case there are any more surprises inside. Looks like it's just a letter, though, with a printed message:

Please excuse the hand-delivered letter, but I promise you I'm someone you can trust. There are several files on this USB stick which should help you out with some of your project work. I understand you're trying to track down a certain individual who won't take kindly to being followed – but let's just say it's in everyone's interests that you keep going, with a view to bringing them down.

On the USB stick is evidence of their less-than-legal activities, plus a few other bits of incriminating data you might want to keep hold of. You'll notice that the files are locked when you open the drive, but I've given you the password to unlock them in this envelope. Make sure you scan everything carefully, and then use every fifth digit.

You'll figure it out.

Best of luck,

A Friend

You read the letter a few times, looking for any other clues, but there's not much else to uncover. The envelope just has one other item inside: a slip of paper with what looks like a distorted barcode on it. What's this for?

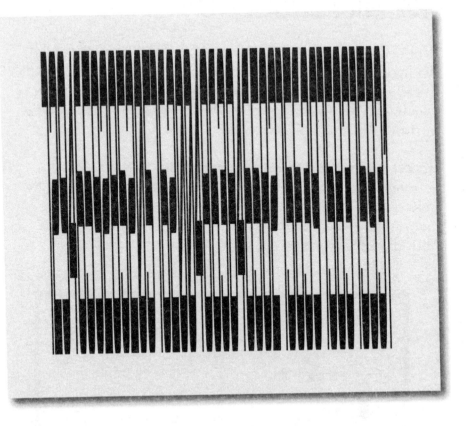

You insert the USB stick and have a flick through the contents. There are multiple folders on the stick but, as promised, they're all password protected. You wrack your brain trying to understand what the message means – and what the sender meant by 'scan everything carefully, then use every fifth digit'.

You twiddle your thumbs, twizzling the barcode paper around in your hands. Then, in a flash of realization, you realize that the secret is simply to look at things from a new angle. **What's the passcode which you need to unlock the files?**

25. Microdots

Not everyone runs a hi-tech operation, and sometimes you find yourself communicating with people via unusual means. It's usually best not to ask too many questions of the people who contact you anonymously, although sometimes you can run into transmission problems.

You've been trying to decrypt some files sent to you via a microdot camera, but you've hit a couple of hitches. Firstly, two crucial images don't seem to give you any helpful information at all. And secondly, apparently you'll need a four-digit passcode to access the next set of files.

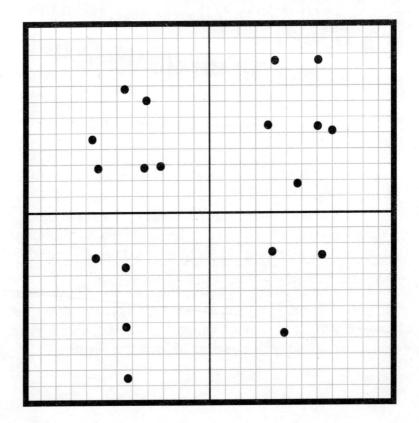

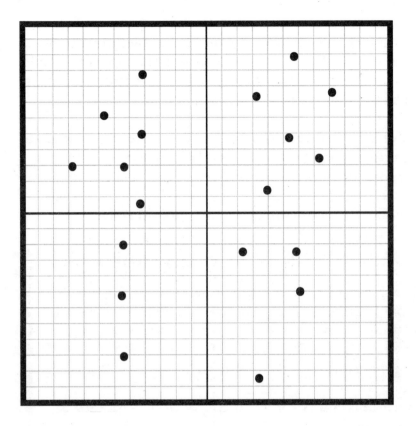

After a while, you realize each image only has half the information you need. **Can you combine the information they contain to find the four digits you need?**

26. Enter at Risk

You've gained access to some top-secret blueprints for a surveillance project. You're planning to pass them onto a client who – for an unknown reason – is hoping to gain access to the buildings someday. Best not to ask too many questions, you find.

The ground floor of each building has been divided into a series of small cubicles and vestibules – probably to give whoever works there a certain amount of privacy from their colleagues. What results, however, is a confusing system of corridors that interconnect in very limited ways.

You've found four floorplans – one for each building. On the four floor maps below, you should be able to enter one side of each building by the door indicated with an arrow, and follow a route to emerge at the exit on the other side through a different door. Something's off, though, since on one of the buildings you can enter on one side but not then exit out of the other side.

Which building is split into two entirely separate ground floor areas?

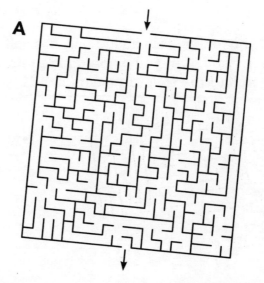

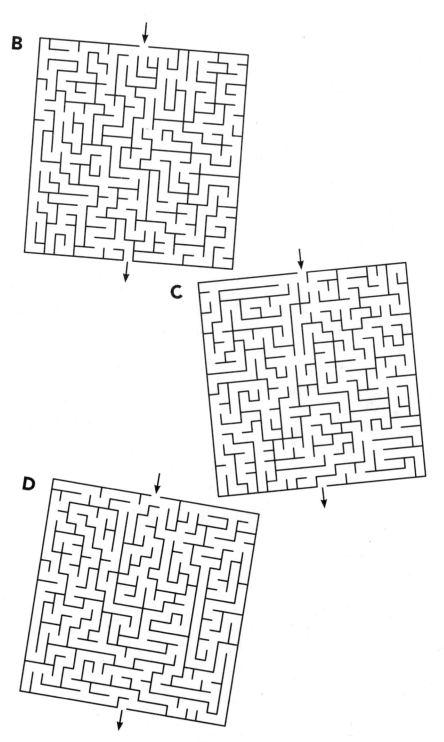

27. Image Issues

You're taking a casual peek through someone's personal files online when you come across the following image, labelled 'Username'. Jackpot!

You've been trying to identify the particular username they use for a few critical online profiles, so perhaps this image will hold the key.

When you open up the image, though, it appears extremely glitchy, and splits into two sections:

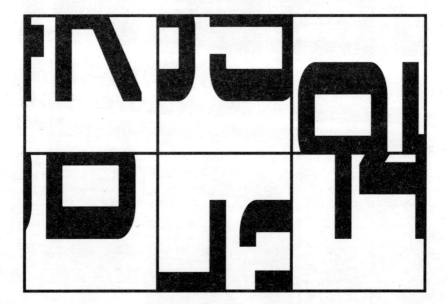

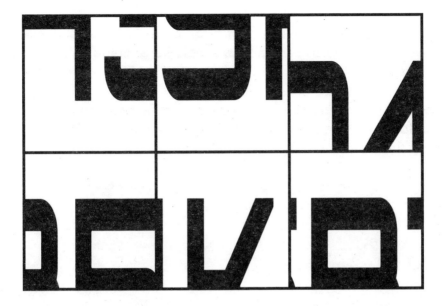

From previous investigation you feel confident that the username should consist of 8 characters. You start by drawing a 6×2 grid to rearrange the 12 image segments into:

Can you redraw the 12 segments (6 per image) in the empty grid above, to reveal the hidden username? You are confident that none of the image segments will need to be rotated or reflected.

28. Crack the Code

You've spent days breaking through a pretty gnarly security system, when you reach a final hurdle in which a four-digit passcode is needed to bring down the last firewall. All you can see on the screen at the moment, however, is a bunch of symbols with numbers beneath – far more than just the four digits which you need:

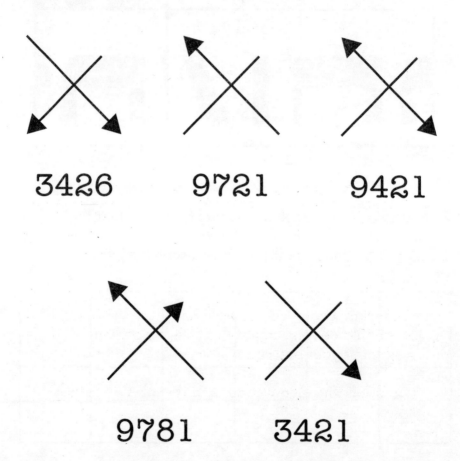

3426   9721   9421

9781   3421

You try entering all five of the different codes shown, but none of them work. There's nothing much to help you out there, and despite a considerable amount of effort you fail to make progress in converting the crossed arrow symbols into digits either.

After a while, however, the following image pops up on the screen, with a prompt beneath:

????

Ah, it seems that you need to work out which four-digit number should be attached to this final crossed-arrow image, and use that as your passcode.

Can you break the arrow code, and reveal the four-digit number?

29. It All Adds Up

You're taking an inventory of your home setup and boy, do you have a lot of kit. You want to replace some of the cables which attach to your devices, but first you need to work out how many cables you have of each type.

Each device in your home setup has exactly two cables attached, leading off to other hardware: one red and one green. The red cables are 2m long, the green cables are 3m long, and each device has exactly one of each cable attached. You decide that all of the red cables need replacing.

If the total length of the green and red cables currently in use is 30m, then **how many devices do you have set up right now, and what is the total length of red cable you will need to replace?**

30. Missing Links

You're used to making connections online, but now you're faced with a different connectivity problem: a circuit board has been delivered which needs various of its components connected together to form a single loop.

On the board below, draw additional lines so that every dot is joined with a horizontal or vertical line to two other dots, to create a single complete loop. The circuit loop cannot cross or touch itself at any point, in case of short circuiting. Some parts of the loop are already given, but the rest is up to you. **Can you finish connecting up the board?**

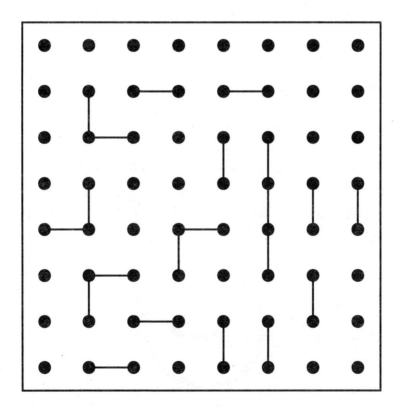

31. Fitting In

You're trying to enter an encrypted chat room, but the security is pretty tight. It's a good sign, because you need to know everything is kept under wraps if you become a member. Nevertheless, it's proving a bit frustrating – you need to get into the chat one way or another.

After your usual shortcuts fail, you get a message from someone you believe is already in the chat room. Here's what they say:

> We see you've been trying to get in for a while. You've passed our initial vetting, but we want to make sure you're the real deal first. We've been caught out before, and can't risk it again.
>
> You need a four-digit code to enter. I've listed some options below. It's one of them.
>
> Check your email. I've sent you an attachment to open which should help you figure out which code you need to use. Most of the four-digit codes fit into the grid reading across or down. But we're looking for people who don't really fit in, so it's the one code that doesn't fit that will let you enter the chat.
>
> Reply to this email with the correct four-digit code and we'll grant access. Send back the wrong code and you'll be blocked for life. Good luck!

Well, that's pretty clear. You don't mind a challenge every now and again. You check the bottom of the message and they've sent the following four-digit codes:

You open up your email inbox and, sure enough, there's a grid image for you to fit some of the numbers into. Looks like they've already placed one of the digits to get you started:

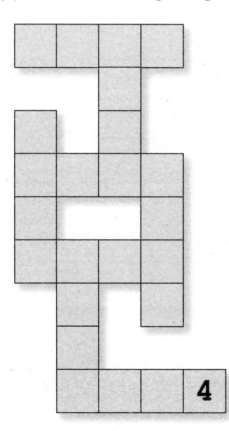

Which is the misfit code, so that you can submit it for entry to the chat room?

32. Through the Keyhole

You're considering taking on some work for a potentially lucrative client, but they want to test your attention to detail before they trust you with any risky business. They've sent over a photograph of a circuit board that they want you to pay close attention to:

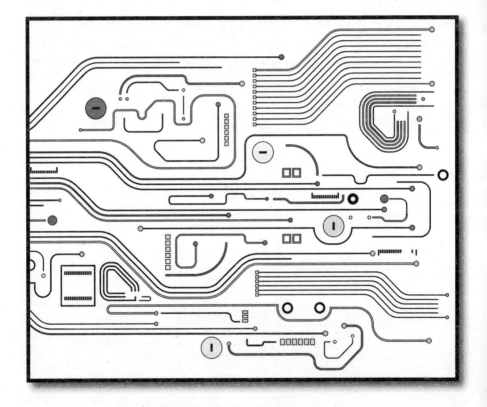

In another message, they send you six additional pictures. It looks, at first glance, like close-up images of the circuit board as seen through a keyhole:

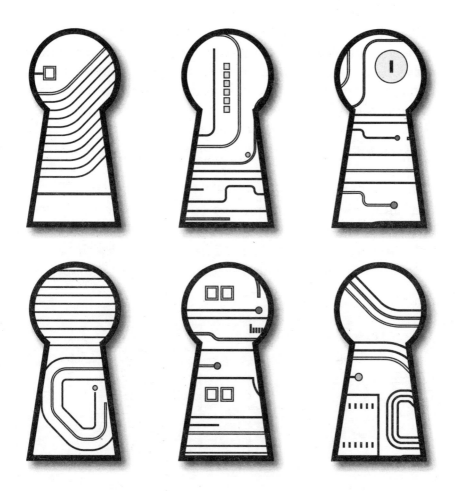

Only one of the keyholes shows an actual close-up of the circuit board, however. **Which one?**

33. Mixed Message

Years ago, you teamed up with a hacker to break into the online security system belonging to a bank. For a while now, you've both been gently skimming money from the savings accounts of the bank's richest customers – not so much that any individual would notice, but enough to keep you both afloat for a while while you're working on other projects. One day, your friend sends you a message via an encrypted chat:

I'm not sure we're flying as far under the radar
as we'd like to. I think the bank might be keeping
tabs on us. For now, I've set up a new account for
the money to go into in case they try to divert it
elsewhere. Here's the six-digit account number:

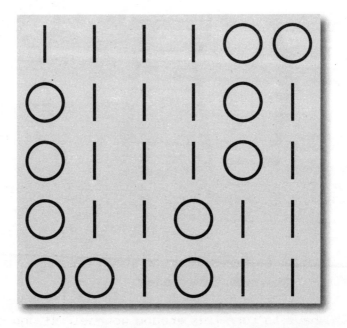

Your friend is usually pretty detailed and thorough, but you've got no idea what this means. Is it binary code? You try out a few of the possible numbers in binary, but it doesn't make any sense. You can't see a way to make six digits with this, and ask your friend what's going on.

They reply with an email, in a secure inbox. This time, it's just a picture of the Morse code for the digits from 0 to 9:

1: ● — — — —
2: ● ● — — —
3: ● ● ● — —
4: ● ● ● ● —
5: ● ● ● ● ●
6: — ● ● ● ●
7: — — ● ● ●
8: — — — ● ●
9: — — — — ●
0: — — — — —

And that doesn't seem to make any sense either – none of the rows match any of the Morse digits in the guide. What's going on?

Finally, you see a message from your friend back in the encrypted chat:

You'll have to turn this around yourself. If you need a clue, the first digit should be 4.

After a while, you do crack their unusual code. **What's the six-digit account number?**

34. Spin Cycle

You've seen some pretty clever ways to protect information online, and this one is certainly creative. Someone you're trying to snoop on has created this safe-style puzzle, which needs a six-digit code to unlock it. And there's no alternative if you want to access their files – you'll have to crack the code.

There's only one way to spin these dials and line up the numbers so that each of the five numbers (reading out from the central ring) has no touching digits with a difference of less than two. 392753 would be valid, but 327844 wouldn't be because the 3 and 2 would be touching, the 7 and 8 would be touching, and the 4 and 4 would be touching.

Spin the dials until all five of the six-digit numbers fulfil this rule. The access code you need is the one starting with '3'. **What is it?**

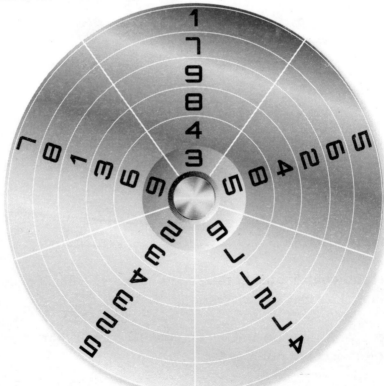

35. Handy Coordination

Every now and again, a hacker gets hacked – the irony!
Someone's decided to target you now, and they've already
gained limited access to your internal network. You could
retaliate, but you've decided to send them a gentle warning:
instead of locating them virtually, you want to show you can
find them geographically.

Hidden in the grid below are the coordinates of their location
somewhere in the world. Place a digit from 1 to 6 into each
empty square, so that no digit repeats in any row, column
or bold-lined 3×2 box. When complete, the shaded row will
reveal the coordinates east reading from left to right, and the
shaded column will reveal the coordinates north reading from
top to bottom. **Where is your hacker hiding?**

3				4	1
1			3		
	2				
				5	
		3			2
2	4				5

Insert the coordinates here:

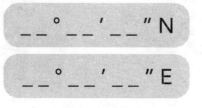

__ ° __ __ ' __ __ " N

__ __ ° __ __ ' __ __ " E

36. QR Query

A vague acquaintance of dubious provenance has sent you a set of QR codes, which they claim lead to various websites where you can invest in lucrative cryptocurrencies. They assure you that none of these websites will be able to track you, copy your data or interfere with your system in any way at all. Sure.

You don't trust this person at all. For a start, they say they've sent you eight different QR codes, but they all look very similar. In fact, two of them are completely identical. **Which two?**

E

F

G

H

Note: These are not functioning QR codes. This puzzle does not require a QR-code scanner.

37. Decisions Decisions

You're thinking of taking on a little extra work to help pay the bills, and have lined up a few potential clients.

You only want to agree to one project, which is made more complex because they're each asking for a different amount of time commitment from you, as well as offering different amounts of pay.

- Client R needs you to work for half of the time that Client Q does.

- Client F wants you to work for them for 10 days.

- Client R is offering the least money.

- Client Q wants you to work for three times as many days as the highest-paying person does.

It's now decision time.

What has each of the clients asked for in terms of your time, and who is willing to pay the most – and the least?

38. Blocked Off

Hacking into cybersecurity is both a science and an art. This time, you'll need to use a little of both to access the files of an architect's firm.

You know that the following image contains clues about a three-digit code you need to access their internal network.

Despite the image looking like a building plan, you know that with this company the key will be a question of perspective.

Can you look at the plan another way and find the three-digit code you need?

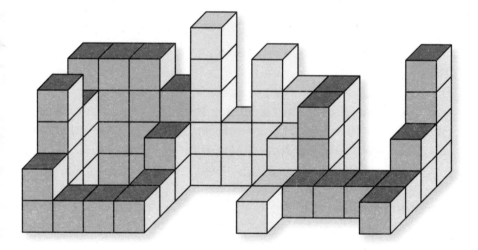

39. Lead the Way

You're waiting on some files from a friend when you receive an email with the following unusual image attached:

X ◀◀◀▲▲▲▲▶▶▶ ▼▼▼▼▼▼

▶▶▶ ▼▼▼ ◀◀◀▶▶ ▼▼▼ ◀◀◀

◀◀◀◀▼▼▼▶▶▶ ▼▼▼ ◀◀◀

▼▼▼▼▼▼▶▶▶ ▲▲▲ ◀◀

That's very weird – no text, no other files, no clues. Your friend is somewhat of a loose cannon who's pretty protective of their online profile, but even for them this is unusual. You print out the image for future reference, just in case you need it. Looks like you'll just have to be patient.

The next day, a second email drops into your inbox. It has the promised files attached, although they're passcode protected. There's also some text, and a pretty sparse picture tagged onto the bottom of the email:

```
Start at 'x', using the previous
image I sent to guide you. Get all
four digits and you're in.
```

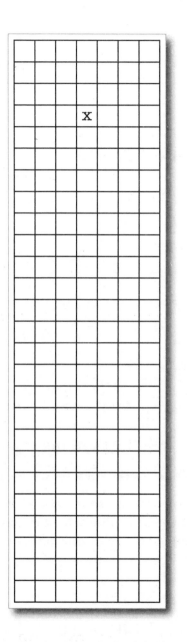

Your friend certainly doesn't like to make it easy. **What's the four-digit passcode?**

40. Skimming Sequence

You may (or may not...) have been using some new wireless software to skim details from credit card transactions that are taking place in your local area. After a while, however, you notice that the numbers you're picking up are starting to look a little suspicious – that is, they don't seem to be genuine card numbers. You think someone might be interfering with your software, and wonder if there's a pattern to the numbers you're receiving.

Here are the last six credit-card numbers your software has picked up:

6121-8243-0364-2485

4812-1620-2428-3236

3691-2151-8212-4273

8162-4324-0485-6647

5101-5202-5303-5404

7142-1283-5424-9566

If your theory is correct – and the card numbers do seem to be forming a pattern – then **which of these four numbers would be the most likely for your software to 'detect' next?**

a. 1234-5678-9012-3456

b. 2468-1012-1416-1820

c. 1112-1314-1516-1718

d. 0102-0304-5060-7080

41. Out of Space

You want to organize your USB sticks, since you have quite a few and it's probably a good idea to keep them in good order considering how much incriminating information they hold – not just on you, but on many other people too.

At the moment you've been keeping them all in a box with a combination lock that only you know the code to. Recently, however, there's been some overspill, and you can't fit them all into one box any more.

After a quick count, you find that there are 16 USB sticks in the overspill pile.

You hunt for a new box and find one which should fit the bill – in fact, it's got 60% more storage space than the previous box. This means you'll be able to fit in all of the USB sticks you currently have, and still have room for 14 more.

How many USB sticks can fit into the box you currently have – and how many USB sticks do you have?

42. Fingerprints

One of your hacker contacts has been leaving fingerprints everywhere – digitally speaking, that is. He's used the image below as a tag on certain websites, to let his followers know where he's been:

You've looked at some of his suspected hackings, however, and there's something funny going on: it turns out that some of the fingerprint images he's left behind don't exactly match the one you know he normally uses.

You've found four different fragments of the supposed fingerprint so far, but only one of them matches your contact's:

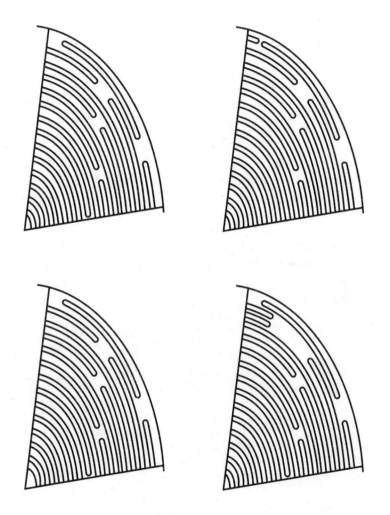

Which one of these fragments is an exact match?

43. The Key

You come home one day to see that someone's let themself into your apartment! You'd better change the locks, and upgrade the alarm system. It seems they haven't taken anything this time, or (looking at the logs) even switched on your computer – but there's a note stuck to your desk:

Give me a call

Dial the numbers on the keys in order

0 means nothing

You look at your computer keypad, and see that they've made a few changes. They've erased all of the labels, apart from on the digit keys which have been rearranged:

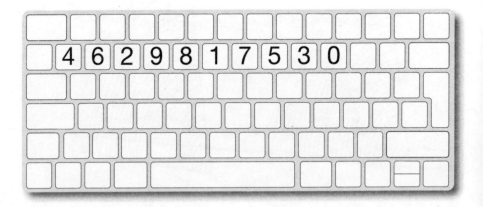

You try calling 462981753 – leaving out the 0 – but no dice. What else could 'in order' mean? **What nine-digit number should you dial?**

44. Hiding Inside

You're working on a joint project with a hacker friend, and you're at the final stage of penetrating an encrypted network. Your buddy needs to switch off for the night, however, so they send over a hint they just unlocked for the final four-digit passcode which you'll need.

Here's their message:

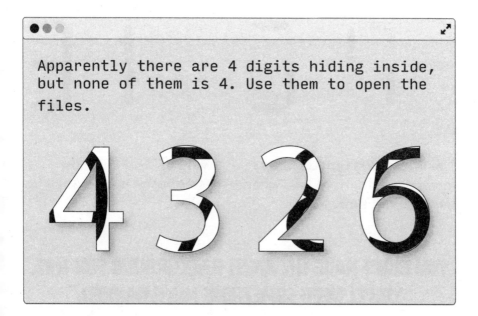

```
Apparently there are 4 digits hiding inside,
but none of them is 4. Use them to open the
files.
```

What four-digit number do you need?

45. Time is Missing

You've been working around the clock to access a network that's going to be shut down very soon.

Just as you're about to break in, you're shown a timestamp that should tell you how many hours, minutes and seconds there are until the whole server self-destructs. Unfortunately, however, it doesn't seem to be complete:

The incomplete image leaves you trying to work out how much time you have left, when a mysterious message pops up beneath the time:

YOU DON'T HAVE THE RIGHT BACKGROUND FOR THIS. YOU'LL NEED SOMETHING MUCH DARKER.

Ignoring the fact that someone seems to have their eye on you, you try and understand their message. Suddenly, you realize you've been looking in the wrong places. **How much time is left?**

46. Journey Jumble

Every now and then, you'll be called upon to do some surveillance work for individuals who want to keep tabs on friends or family.

Recently you've been following someone around the world – virtually, of course – and trying to work out where they'll be jetting off to next. From their social media posts, it sounds like their next trip will be a long one, and a quick snoop through their email inbox reveals a folder called 'Itinerary'. That should be a big clue!

When you open the emails, however, you don't see the place names you expect to, which should each be one word long. All of the names seem to be scrambled, in fact. **Can you work out which eight capital cities your international voyager is heading off to next?**

SLOBIN

BADSTEPUP

ATATOW

SHINLIKE

BRANRACE

SPAREGOIN

ROBINIA

RATAJAK

47. Set the Bar

You think someone is trying to communicate with you using barcodes as a way to transmit numbers – but you've used a barcode scanner and no numbers are popping out. Maybe it's a waste of time, but you're curious to know what this person is after. It looks like they want to test you first to see if you can help them, because they've sent you a challenge.

The four barcodes below were all sent in one attachment. The sender assures you that the four images are connected in some way, and there's a hidden number sequence in each one:

You spend some time looking at the barcodes to try and discover the patterns you're presumably looking for – and eventually you realize what they all have in common. After a while, however, you receive another message. They've sent you four more barcodes, and some text:

Consider this an expression of interest, from both sides. If you respond correctly to this message, then I'll know you're serious about talking more.

Only one of these barcodes is similar to the first four. Can you work out which one it is? Hope you've been paying attention... so reply with the number in the top-left corner of the barcode you choose.

Assuming that you want to carry on communicating, which barcode fits with the others? **And so which number should you reply with?**

48. Go With the Flow

You're trying to access an online server when you hit a (virtual) wall. You were expecting to be sent a four-digit code to move to the next stage, but instead you get this flow chart:

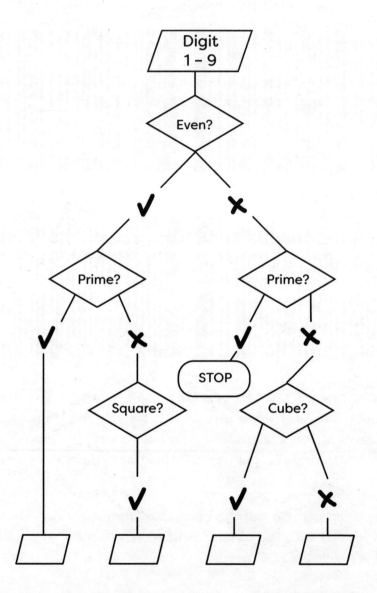

Can you go with the flow and figure out the four-digit code?

49. Key Problem

You've been sent a bunch of keys in the mail – one of which you believe opens a real-life padlocked safe you need access to. They're almost identical, but only one of them matches the lock. For complex reasons, you can only bring one with you to try at the safe – but luckily you do have an image of the correct key to help you narrow it down.

Allowing for reflection and rotation, **which is the only smaller key that exactly matches the larger one at the top left?**

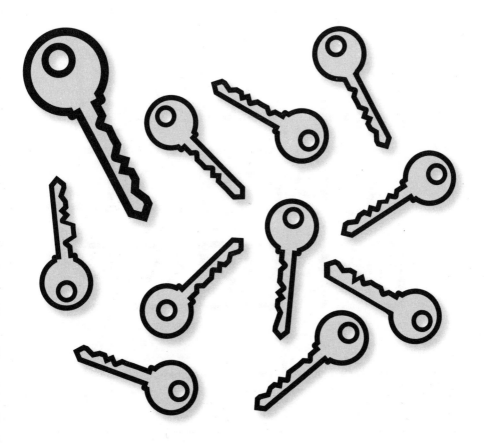

50. Going Back in Time

You're looking at some security footage online when you notice that the timestamps of some images look a little off.

These four times should be listed in chronological order, using a 24-hour clock:

$$55:02:\text{HE}$$

$$1J:38:00$$

$$15:23:18$$

$$01:08:52$$

Can you work out what's gone wrong, and what the correct timestamps should be?

51. Caught in the Web

A potential client has been in touch, and wants to know how good you are at analysing numbers quickly. They've sent over the image below, and want you find the only way of travelling from '1' to '9' in numeric order, using only the given lines between numbers and always stepping to a higher value after each move.

Can you spot the chain?

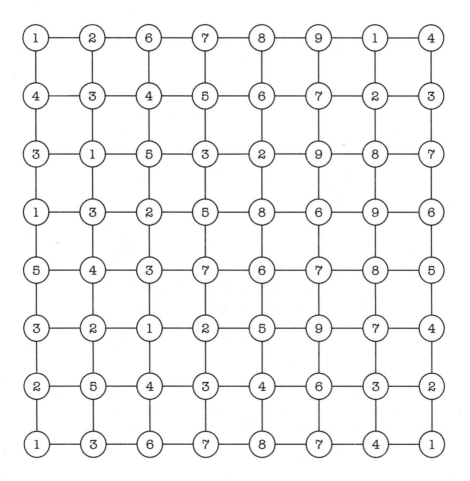

52. Dial It In

A contact has a physical hard drive that they want you to break into, which they have left in a safe in a city bank. You know you'll need a six-digit number to access the safe, but the only information they've sent you – via email – is the following image, without explanation:

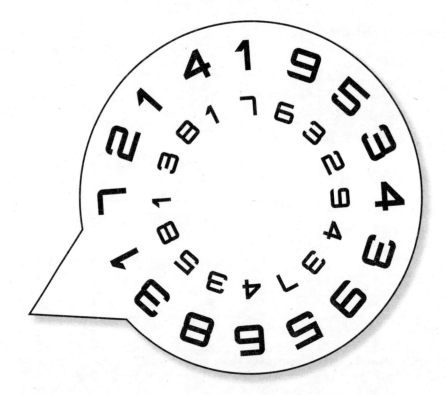

It doesn't make any sense on its own, but later on you receive the following image in a different inbox, with the subject line 'Order from largest to smallest':

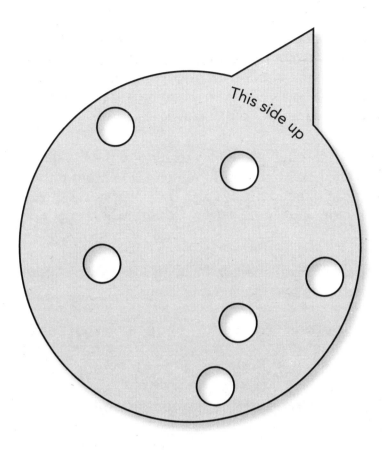

What's the six-digit number that you need?

53. It's a Date

You're trying to disable a security system, but you can't complete the process without a four-digit kill code. You believe that the code corresponds to a date in the format D/M/YY (with one digit for the day, and one for the month), but that doesn't sufficiently narrow down the options for you.

You search through some files relating to the building's occupants, hoping to find something significant to point you in the right direction. You don't find any dates, but you do spot a folder labelled 'Security Codes', which might be a winner.

You open a folder labelled 'Building Alarm', which turns out to contain one text file and one image:

Instructions for kill code extraction:

1. Only to be used as a last resort.

2. Shade some grid squares according to the given clue numbers.

3. The clues provide, in reading order from left to right or top to bottom, the length of every run of consecutive shaded squares in each row and column.

4. There must be a gap of at least one empty square between each run of shaded squares in the same row or column.

5. Read resulting image numbers left to right, top to bottom.

6. You will have ONE attempt at the code.

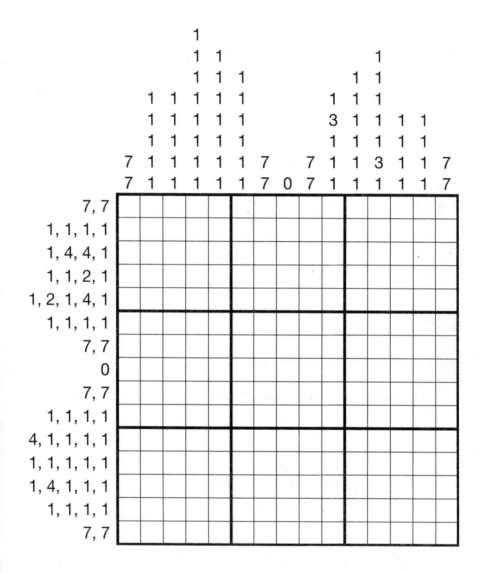

What code will you need?

54. Attachment Issues

Someone has sent you an email with three attachments, each of a different size.

You know that one of the attachments contains information you need if you want to make progress in your current project, but the dodgy sender is not to be trusted – and in particular you know that the other two attachments are likely to contain viruses that could totally destroy your setup.

As a gesture of goodwill, they've set up a game of logic which should – if you get it right – help you work out which of the attachments is safe to open. They've hidden the individual file sizes from you, but they have sent the following clues:

- The Blue file is exactly half the size of one of the other files

- The file labelled Green is 4MB in size

- The Red file is one-and-a-half times the size of the smallest file

- One of the attachments is 3MB in size

- Only attachments with a size that is an odd number of MB are safe to open

While file, or files, is safe to open?

55. Missing Pieces

You need some upgrades to your home system, so you have ordered a shipment of hardware that should arrive any day now.

Before the delivery arrives, however, you receive an invoice that doesn't look correct, with half of the information missing.

In the list of computer parts below, **can you fill in the gaps – one letter per gap – to complete the set of items?**

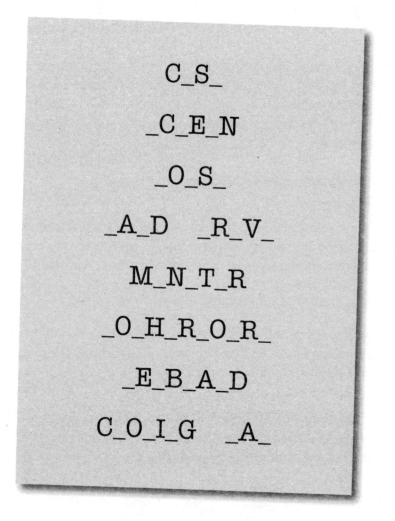

C_S_

_C_E_N

_O_S_

_A_D _R_V_

M_N_T_R

_O_H_R_O_R_

_E_B_A_D

C_O_I_G _A_

56. The Motherboard

You've followed a few online courses on electronics, and have decided you want to try your hand at routing a circuit board of your own. Over time, you want to learn how to create an entire motherboard from scratch, but for now you'll just have a go at the basics.

You've done your preparation and already know in advance which sections of the board need to be wired to others in the circuit, so you just need to plan out an efficient way of connecting these various sections. You decide to draw out a sketch of the route around the board that you have in mind.

The block-diagram plan of the circuit board shown opposite is split up by the bold lines into different sections. Each of these sections – and all of the smaller squares within – needs to be connected into the circuit so as to form a single loop which joins them all.

Specifically, you need to plan out the board by:

- Drawing a single loop which visits every square of the circuit board exactly once, without revisiting any square (which also means the loop cannot cross over itself).

- Only joining squares horizontally or vertically.

- Aiming for an efficient system, so the loop can only enter and exit each bold-lined region once – once it leaves it, it can't return.

So far, so simple. **Can you follow the instructions and complete the plan of the circuit board**, before you then proceed to try and make the real thing?

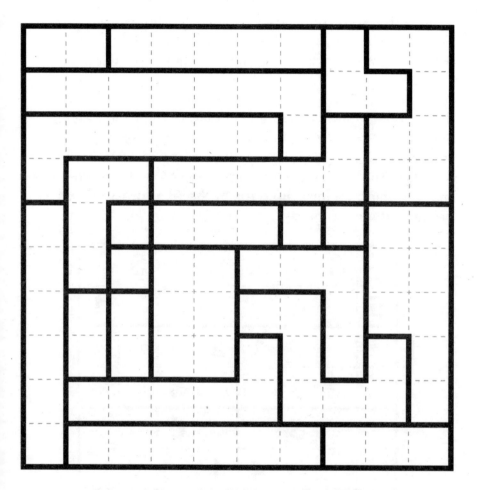

57. Addressing the Problem

You've been trying to block the IP address of a rogue device that is sabotaging your internal network. Unfortunately you're being overwhelmed with log data, so you'll need to pick out the correct number from the partially empty grid below.

To reveal the IP address, however, which in this consists of four two-digit numbers, you'll need to think logically to uncover it. Place a digit from 1 to 8 into each empty square, so that no digit repeats in any row, column or bold-lined 4×2 box. Then, once you're done, **insert the digits from the shaded diagonal into the gaps in the IP address shown below**, with one digit per gap, reading from left to right.

	8					3	
5		4			8		1
			1	2			
	7			5			
	8			6			
		4	1				
8	6				7		3
	5					6	

IP address: _ _ . _ _ . _ _ . _ _

58. Fickle Friend

You've asked a hacker friend to help you out on a project and, at last, they have managed to get hold of the six-digit passcode you need to access a particular set of files. When they send the passcode over and you take a look, however, it looks like they've decided to have a bit of fun.

The numbers you need have been written as words and then split into multiple fragments. Those fragments have been sorted into alphabetical order.

Work out which six digits have been broken up below and then write out the completed words in increasing order of value to obtain the code you need. Each fragment is used exactly once. **What is the code?**

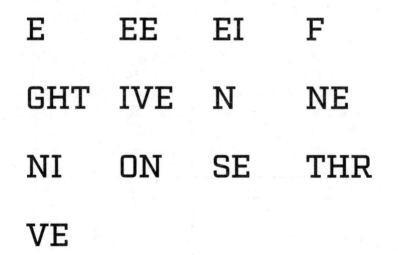

59. Meet in the Middle

You're meeting up with a friend to hand over a hard drive which contains some files that neither of you would want to be caught with. Exchanging the drive face-to-face somehow seems lower risk than sending files online – plus it's a huge amount of data that would be sure to draw attention.

You agree to meet your friend in a spot somewhere between your two 'offices'. Today you'll deliver the hard drive, with all the files on it – and then tomorrow they'll hand it back to you, in person, with the incriminating files replaced with pictures of fluffy bunnies. Or something like that.

You've not only agreed on the locations but also on a precise route between your two offices which you'll both stick to, and which will remain exactly the same on both days. That way you're then guaranteed to bump into each other at some point on the route, where you can exchange drives and then return immediately back by retracing your steps.

Using your pedometer, you note that you transported the hard drive 1,200m from your office to the pickup-point on the first day, and then your friend of course took it the rest of the way to their office. The next day, you walked at different speeds and so the exact location of the drop-off point changed – this time it was 1,800m away from your friend's office. You didn't want to get caught by using the same drop-off point twice.

Once the handover was complete and you were back in your home setup with the 'clean' hard drive, you begin to wonder: **which one of you physically walked a greater distance, and by how much further?**

60. Chain Mail

A few weeks ago you sent out a spam email as part of an experiment: you wanted to track its progress round the world, and see who was sending it on. Attaching a bit of spyware to the email was easy, as an extra bonus. The email was designed in such a way that it could only be forwarded in its original form to exactly one person, whose next forward you could then track from a distance. This morning someone sent it to you – not knowing you were the source – and completed the loop.

Now comes the fun part: mapping out where the email has been. All of the dots below are recipients of the email, starting with you in the top left. **Can you join all of the participants into a single loop, tracking the email's progress as you go?** The loop cannot cross or touch itself at any point. Only horizontal and vertical lines between dots are allowed. Some parts of the loop are already given.

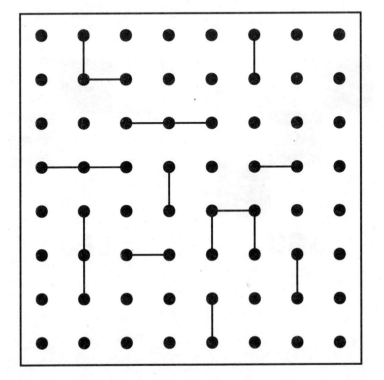

61. Pixel Problem

Like any security-conscious hacker, you have a camera attached to your doorbell. No one knows your true address – well, except for the mail guy – but it's useful in case someone strange comes knocking.

Recently, you've noticed that someone new has been hanging around. They come over every day, ring the doorbell, look into the camera, and leave. Not suspicious at all! Your camera is programmed to take a picture of anyone who comes to the door and save it into a folder, so you are certain it's the same person each day.

You begin to wonder who else is showing up at your door, and decide to take a proper look at the pictures to see what you can find. When you open the folder, however, there's an immediate problem – every photo has changed into a weird pixellated graphic with an error code directly beneath:

369

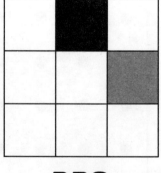

328

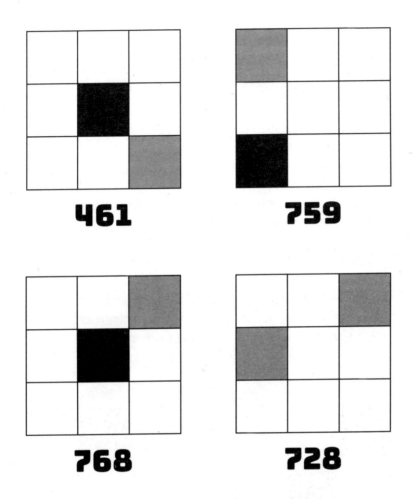

461

759

768

728

What's going on? You don't like this at all.

Minutes later, your computer beeps: someone's emailed you.

Hi there - hope you haven't minded me stopping
by, but it wasn't that tricky to work out
where you live. As you can see, it's not too
hard to find you both online and in real life.
It was also pretty easy to get rid of the
photos you've been taking of me. You invade my
privacy, and I'll invade yours.

I want a truce. You've been looking into my systems recently and I don't like it. Consider this a warning: keep snooping and I'll wipe everything you have. Leave me alone and I'll leave you alone.

I've uploaded one more image for you, to the folder where you've been keeping the pictures. And no, it's not blank. I've chosen that image for a reason. Figure out the error code that should go beneath. If you reply to this email with the correct code, the truce is on. If not - well, you know what I plan to do. The choice is yours. Choose wisely.

This isn't good – you've been mixed up with some shady people before and who knows what they might do if pushed. At the very least, you can buy some time with a truce while you try and figure out who you've upset this time.

Here's the image they uploaded:

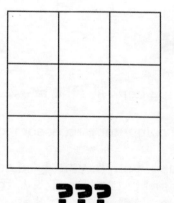

???

They said it's not just 'blank', so there must be meaning to those empty squares. **Can you figure out the three-digit code and send it back to them, before they take drastic action?**

62. More Missing Pieces

You've ordered some more hardware for your home computing system: just a few upgrades as a reward for your own hard work. On the list you are sent just before the delivery, however, there's some information missing.

Specifically, every other letter is missing from the list of computer accessories that you ordered on the invoice below. **Can you fill in the gaps, one letter per gap, to restore the names of the items that are hopefully on their way to you right now?**

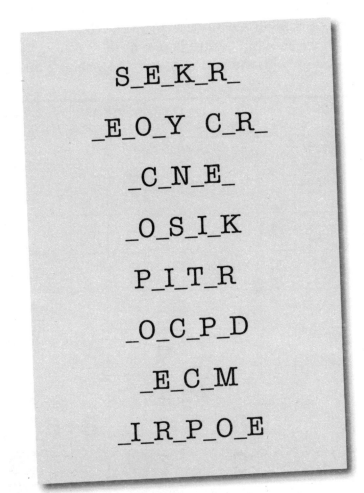

S_E_K_R_

_E_O_Y C_R_

_C_N_E_

_O_S_I_K

P_I_T_R

_O_C_P_D

_E_C_M

_I_R_P_O_E

63. To Your Own Devices

You're trying to back up each of your physical devices online, but with each device having its own separate digital cloud storage. After all, you don't want to have all your information stored in the same place, as you'd be vulnerable if someone managed to access it.

In the grid below, each identical pair of numbers needs to be linked. One of the numbers in each pair represents a physical device, while the other in the pair is its online backup cloud. **Draw a series of separate paths, each connecting a device to a cloud.** No more than one path can enter any square, and paths can only travel horizontally or vertically between squares. Paths shouldn't cross one another – you wouldn't want to end up with the wrong files in the wrong cloud.

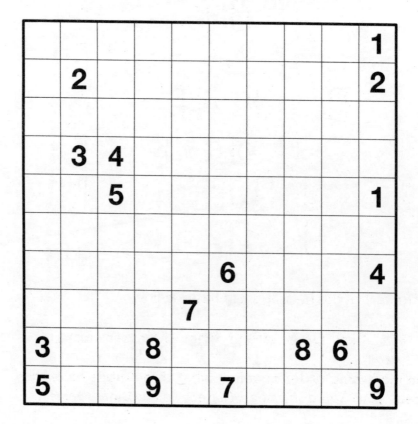

64. The Lighter Ones

You've been trying to team up with a mysterious online group – and when they finally get back to you, they send a puzzle to test you. According to their instructions, there are three digits hidden in the image below – beyond the obvious '0's and '1's, that is. It looks like some kind of binary code:

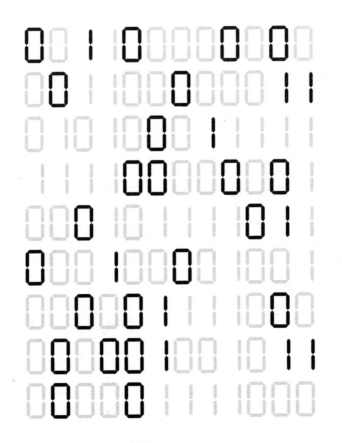

The rest of the message just has one line:

We use only the lighter ones

In increasing order of value, what three digits have they sent you? You don't need to decode any binary values.

65. It's Who You Know

You may have your own network of hackers that you trust, but you think another one is trying to recruit you. This new group, however, don't seem like a good crowd to get mixed up in. At the very least, you need to work out how they're all connected before you respond. Each circled number below is one hacker in the network, and the number indicates how many other hackers you think they're closely connected to.

Join hackers with horizontal or vertical lines to map out the connections. No more than two lines may join any pair of hackers, and no lines may cross. Double lines between a pair of hackers mean they're thick as thieves, and each hacker must have as many lines connected to them as specified by their value. The finished layout must connect all hackers, so you can move between any pair of hackers by following one or more lines. **Can you draw in all the connections?**

94

66. Foreign Friends

You've been working online with some trusted fellow hackers for a few months now. You'd love to call them friends but, the hard truth is, you hardly know anything about them. It's probably good that you all keep yourselves to yourselves, but given that you're curious you decide to do a bit of snooping.

You check the IP address of some of your 'friends' to see which countries they're located in – or at least, the ones they appear to be in when they're online. For some reason the names of the eight countries are showing up in a strange way, however. **Can you work out which one-word country names have had their letters jumbled below?**

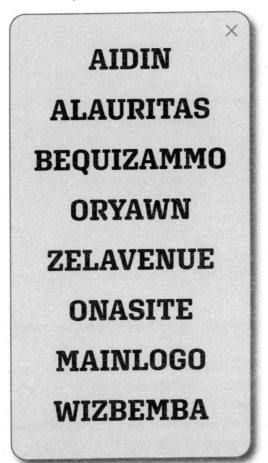

×

AIDIN

ALAURITAS

BEQUIZAMMO

ORYAWN

ZELAVENUE

ONASITE

MAINLOGO

WIZBEMBA

67. Crypto Contest

You've been gaming online with a hacker friend who you've learned you can trust, and who you know has invested in an interesting new cryptocurrency. It's never possible to know what's going to take off and what will fail in the crypto world (although let's be honest – most fail), but after expressing some interest to your friend they make you a playful bet. Here's what your friend offers:

I've got one coin of this new cryptocurrency to offer to you, which you can win in a game of chance. Here's how:

In the real world, I have four fake coins and four real coins – all of the same size and weight, and visually identical.

The coins are in two piles on the table – one of fake and one of real coins – and I have two bags which you can split them up into. You can choose which coins go in which bag. Once each coin is in one of the two bags, we'll toss another coin to decide on one bag for me to take a coin from – and if I then (by chance) pull out a real coin you can have the crypto coin.

This is a fair game. I can't tell by touch or sight what the difference between the coins is, once they're in the bags.

On the face of it this sounds like a 50:50 chance of winning the crypto coin, but after thinking about it for a while you realize it's a sweet deal. **What strategy gives you the best chance of pulling out a real coin? With an optimal strategy, what is your chance of winning?**

68. Ones and Zeros

You've been searching through some databases using raw binary code. Somewhere, the code used is causing a glitch, and it's stopping you from being able to use an important utility.

You're looking for a particular sequence hidden in a huge file, but you've finally narrowed it down to a smaller area, shown below. **Can you find the string '1010101010' hidden in the grid?** It might read in any direction, including backwards and/or diagonally.

1	1	0	1	0	0	0	0	0	1	1	0	1	0	1
1	0	0	0	0	1	1	0	1	1	0	0	0	0	1
0	1	1	0	1	0	1	0	0	0	1	0	1	0	0
0	0	0	0	1	0	0	0	0	1	1	0	0	0	1
0	1	1	0	0	0	1	0	0	1	0	0	0	0	1
1	0	0	1	0	1	1	0	0	0	0	1	0	0	0
1	0	0	1	0	0	0	1	0	1	0	1	0	0	0
0	0	1	0	0	1	0	1	0	0	1	0	1	1	0
0	0	1	0	1	1	0	0	0	0	1	0	1	0	0
0	0	0	0	1	0	0	0	1	0	0	0	0	1	0
1	0	1	0	0	1	0	1	1	0	0	1	0	1	0
0	1	1	0	0	1	0	0	0	1	0	1	0	0	1
0	1	0	1	1	0	1	1	0	1	0	0	1	0	1
0	0	1	0	0	1	0	0	0	0	1	1	0	0	0
1	0	1	0	0	1	0	0	1	0	0	1	0	1	1

69. Speed Search

You're about to gain access to an encrypted surveillance network, when you realize you need a four-digit code to get in. Your software throws up the following suggestions, and you have just thirty seconds to decide on which one to use, with only one attempt possible.

You know the system will be protected by something unique, so you're looking for the only four-digit number where each of the digits is shared by exactly one other number in the set.

How quickly can you find it, and use it to gain access?

1873

7329

4960

5134

1479

9740

8265

7134

1349

70. Pyramid Scheme

You've been lurking online in the background of a mysterious group which is making a lot of money, fast. You're pretty sure it's not entirely legal – which isn't really your concern – but you want to know how they're doing it. When you finally access some of their financial accounts, you see a weird pyramid graphic repeated all over the database; in some of them the boxes are filled, whereas others have blank squares.

Each member of the group seems to have one of these pyramids assigned to them and, by the looks of it, the number on each brick is the total of the two bricks beneath it. You're pretty spooked when you see your own name in the database, with the following – mostly empty – image:

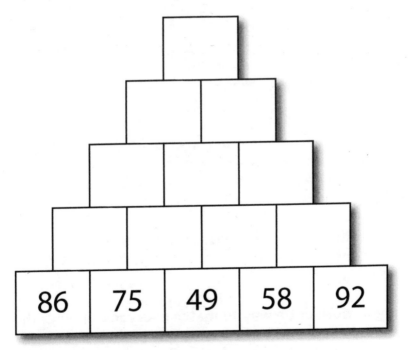

Looks like you didn't stay in the background as much as you had hoped. **If you complete your pyramid in the same way as the others in the database, what will be the number at the top?**

71. They've Got Mail

You've taken on quite a bit of extra client work recently to help pay the bills. Most of the work has involving acting like a private investigator, tracking down people's online profiles.

Sometimes people are looking for incriminating evidence, and sometimes they want a few credit-card numbers, but often enough they're just plain snooping. It's usually best if you don't ask too many questions and try to keep your nose out of the whys and wherefores.

After a busy week, you need to make sure you're sending out the right data to the right clients – giving anyone access to someone else's files could end in disaster.

You've numbered your cases from 1 to 10, to avoid using any direct names, and now it's time to give your customers what they want. To do so, you need to map out the virtual paths between you and your clients.

Draw a series of separate paths, each connecting a pair of identical numbers in the grid – in each pair, one number is you and the other is a client. No more than one path can enter any square, and paths can only travel horizontally or vertically between squares.

It goes without saying that none of the paths between you and a client should ever cross another path – or you'll all be in trouble.

Can you work out a way to match everyone up with the files they need, without crossing any paths?

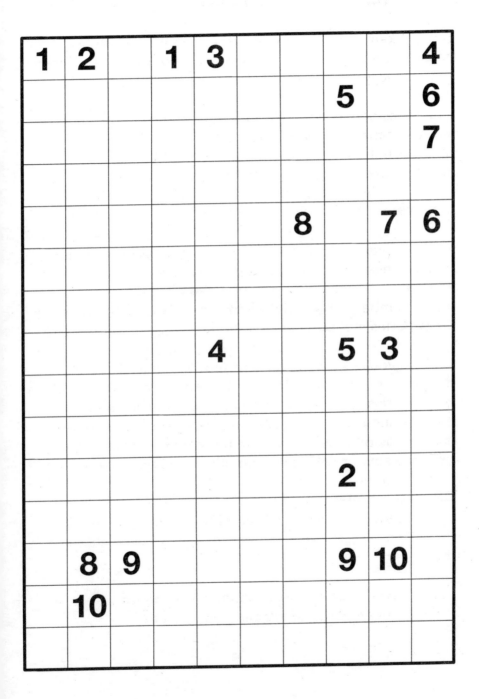

72. Hacking Network

You've set up a small network of hackers whom you trust – or at least up to a point, anyway. As the de facto leader of the group, you're putting together a map of who knows who in the network. It will help you keep tabs on the other members, and allow you to contain the damage quickly in case anyone goes rogue.

In your prototype map, opposite, each of the numbers represents a hacker. Some of them only know a few of the other members, while others are really well-connected.

You need to map out who's linked to other people in the network, drawing lines to connect them. Not only that but you want to keep a note of those who are especially well acquainted, so draw two lines to join pairs of hackers who know each other particularly well.

Join the hackers only with horizontal or vertical lines. No more than two lines may join any pair of hackers, and no lines cross over either each other or another hacker. Each hacker must have as many lines connected as specified by their value. The finished layout must connect all hackers, so you can travel between any pair of hackers by following one or more lines.

Can you complete the map?

3 4 6 4
2 2 1 2
1 2
4 6 3 4
6 2 3 4 2
2 4
4 5 7 4
2 2 2 2 3
2
1 4 4
3 5 5 4 2
2 2 3
4 2 2
3 2
3 4 1
2 1 4 3
3 5 3 1

73. Number Plates

You've been carefully scrolling through the results from a number-plate recognition camera to try and track down a target. You've narrowed down the options to produce these seven possible number plates – all of which are fraudulent:

AE86 BXM

MR27 HFZ

JK90 YWL

VT59 OPL

TY78 QSJ

RW39 KDS

DF42 GCW

You have a friend in law enforcement – always handy – and ask if they can give you some pointers on which of them might be your target. Annoyingly, your friend just sends a very similar list back, with an additional note:

CR27 HFZ
DF45 GCW
JL9O YWL
RW39 KDF
TY78 QRJ
AE86 JXM
VT29 OPL

You get that they have to keep a low profile, but you'd hoped for a bit more help here.

Can you figure out what your friend means, with their almost-identical list? **What are the actual contents of the number plate you need to look for?**

74. Phone a Friend

A client has asked you to find an old friend of theirs, and you're more than happy to oblige.

You find the target's online profile easily enough, but the person you're working for would like their phone number too. You just need to find nine digits.

There are several possibilities to work though, but your client has given you a few clues based on what they can remember.

For a start, they've given you this cryptic number grid to help you figure it out. In fact, your client has already filled in a few digits – but it's up to you to fill in the rest.

Place a digit from 1 to 9 into each of the empty squares in the grid, so that no digit repeats in any row, column or bold-lined 3×3 box. The missing phone number will then be revealed in the shaded diagonal, reading from top to bottom.

What's the phone number that you need?

	4						6	
6		1				4		3
	3		2		4		7	
		5		4		2		
			6		1			
		7		8		5		
	2		4		6		9	
4		6				8		7
	7						4	

75. Code-crack Hackers

Just before you shut everything down for the night, an email drops into one of your more secure mailboxes, from a sender you don't recognize. It reads as follows:

> Hey there. We've noticed you online, and we're sure you've noticed us. We like your work, and we want you to join with us on a few upcoming projects.
>
> We've been following you online for a while and you're clearly competent, although some of your security systems seem a little weak and could use some work. If you don't believe us, just check your last five sent emails. Notice anything fun?
>
> Attached to this email is a little test for you. Pass the test and we'll tell you more – and give you access to a portion of our exploit database you clearly aren't aware of. Trust us when we say we'll make it worth your while.
>
> If you're interested in joining us, reply with the correct three-letter code once you've figured it out. And if we don't hear from you, that's fine – you're either not brave enough, or not smart enough...
>
> Bye for now.

You check your recent sent messages from this server – which you thought was completely secure – and discover that they've added a little smiley face to each of your last five email signatures. How on earth did they manage that?

But you can worry about that later. For now, you want to see if you can work out the code they're asking you for. Here's the image they've included at the bottom of their email:

???

And here's the larger image attachment they included:

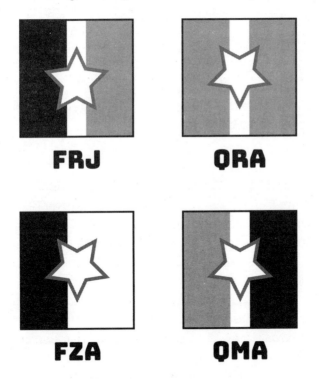

FRJ

QRA

FZA

QMA

You're not sure whether you want to join forces with these dubious characters, but you want to give yourself the opportunity either way. **What is the three-letter code they are expecting?**

76. Around the Houses

Home security systems are usually pretty easy to hack into, meaning you can keep an eye on the houses of wealthy individuals while they naively think they're the only ones checking in. There are a few famous faces you sometimes snoop on just for fun, but one day you notice that a hacker is trying to gain virtual access to *your* security system – the cheek! What are they up to?

You look back at the records, and notice that they have been snooping on eight other different houses, in eight different cities, not including your own house. In fact, they've looked at them all today. From the disordered records, can you figure out which order they snooped on these eight houses in, from first (1) to most recent (8)?

Once you've figured it out, write the order they visited the houses in the gaps below:

1. _____

2. _____

3. _____

4. _____

5. _____

6. _____

7. _____

8. _____

The records let you work out that:

- The property in Boston was not the penultimate location they snooped on

- The Toronto house was looked at immediately after the Malibu house

- They checked in on the Seattle house immediately after they monitored the Boston property

- The Cancun house was the fourth property they snooped on today

- They looked at the Miami house later than they looked at the property in Houston, but not immediately afterwards

- They checked in on the Cancun house before the Seattle house, but not immediately before

- They looked at the Malibu house immediately after the Chicago property

- They looked in on the Toronto house before the Miami house, but not immediately before

77. Back to Front

Your hacker friend – the one who you've been skimming money from bank accounts with (see '33. Mixed Message' on page 52) – needs to send you some new bank details. You've stopped using your old account – they were right, there was definitely somebody sniffing around – and are using a new one using the account number they sent you.

Since then, you've set up another layer of authentication together, making sure that you two – and only you two – can access the account when you need it. In fact, your friend is going to send you a five-digit pin code that they've chosen, meaning you can both have access whenever you want.

Your friend is a little paranoid – although probably quite reasonably so – and once again has sent you an unusual image, instead of just typing out the numbers you need:

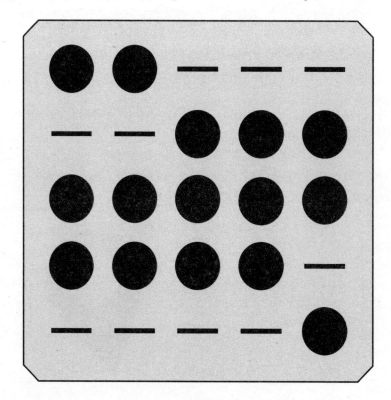

Looks like they're using the Morse code they sent you last time again? At least you still have the handy number guide they sent previously, and you skip back to find it.

Once you enter the access code, however, you get an error message stating that only one of the digits is correct. What? You followed the guide they sent you last time, and they haven't used the same image manipulation trick this time.

You try again – but the number you entered is still not allowed, and it says you have one attempt left before your account is blocked. Knowing your friend, you don't want to let that happen.

You send your friend a message:

> What's going on? I tried the code 27549 but it didn't work, and I used your guide from last time. Help! Don't want to be locked out.

You wait few minutes, and your friend finally replies:

> EGASSEM SIHT DAER DLUOW UOY EKIL SREBMUN EHT DAER DNA - NIAGA YRT

Your friend doesn't really need to worry about anyone else hacking in, because you can barely understand the system yourself. Nevertheless, you realize you've been looking at the numbers from the wrong angle again.

Can you decipher their cryptic clue and work out the five-digit passcode? Which was the only correct digit from your first two attempts?

78. Form of Address

You're trying to track someone down online, and you want to know where in the world they are. They're a slippery customer, and make sure they never connect from the same IP address twice. You feel that it shouldn't be difficult to work out where they are, but somehow they keep getting away from you. Frustrating.

You've been keeping a record of the IP addresses they've used in the past few months, wondering if there's a pattern since it seems they are spoofing them. After all, if they're choosing new addresses, they might have a system in place to create a new one.

Here's the list they've used so far this week:

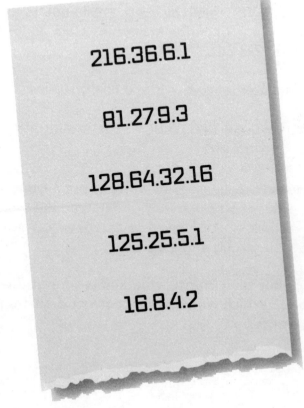

216.36.6.1

81.27.9.3

128.64.32.16

125.25.5.1

16.8.4.2

You decide to run the numbers through some pattern-recognition software to see what it discovers. It throws up a few suggestions for possible other IP addresses that your target might use next, although it doesn't tell you outright what any pattern might be.

Here's the list of possible next IP addresses that your software has come up with:

A. 121.11.2.1

B. 2.4.6.8

C. 111.222.333.444

D. 123.124.125.126

E. 144.121.100.81

F. 1.1.1.1

G. 216.125.64.27

H. 17.11.7.5

When compared to the list opposite, there's one address that you realize immediately would fit with the way the others have been chosen. **Which one?**

79. Blueprint Blues

You've hacked into the surveillance system of a building compound downtown, which may or may not be of some significance to the government. Based on information gained from the cameras, you've put together two approximate floorplans for two different units – which again may or may not be of interest to a client of yours, whose name you'll be keeping under wraps.

You've drawn a rough sketch from the data you have – one floorplan for each building. Your data isn't quite complete but, from what you can see, the two ground floor areas are different shapes overall and divided into various rooms. They also both have exactly one room which is a perfect square – although the rest of your sketches are not quite to scale.

Here's the sketch you have of Unit A, and the measurements you've worked out so far:

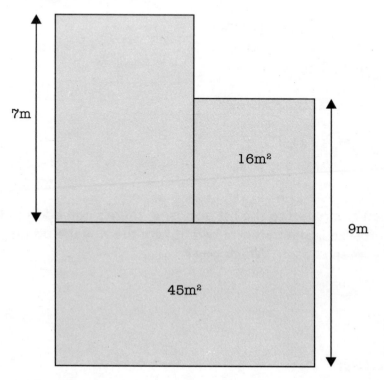

And here's what you have for Unit B, which has one additional room compared to Unit A:

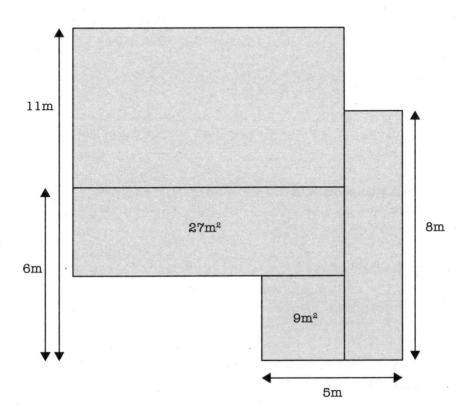

If your data is going to be of use to anyone, it needs to be accurate and complete. **Which of the two floorplans shows the largest overall area?** Assume that all the rooms are perfect squares or rectangles, and all walls measure a whole number of metres.

80. Room for One More

You're trying to track down a hacker that you think might be encroaching on your activities, and possibly even working in the same physical area as you. You've tracked their online movements to a hotel nearby, and after looking at the security footage you reckon you've got your guy.

You want to deliver a message in person without revealing too much about yourself. There's a hitch though – the CCTV footage is so grainy that you can't see the exact number of the room they're in, and it's not like you can safely call the hotel and ask.

You take a blurred screen grab of the door you need, and try to generate a clearer picture manually, based on the pixel information on the image.

Using the following rules and the grid opposite, **can you process the image and work out the number written on the door of your rival's hotel room?**

1. Shade some grid squares according to the given clue numbers.

2. The clues provide, in reading order from left to right or top to bottom, the length of every run of consecutive shaded squares in each row and column.

3. There must be a gap of at least one empty square between each run of shaded squares in the same row or column.

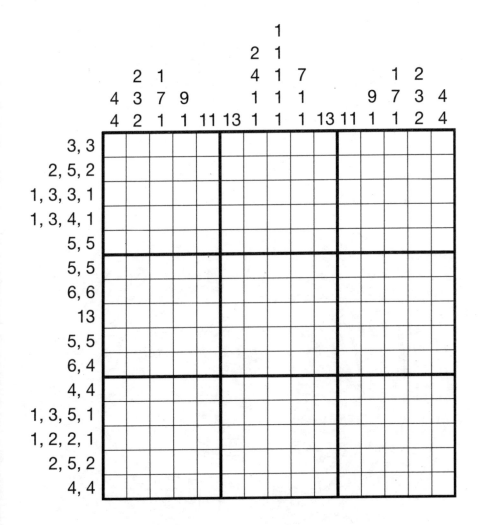

81. Bit Suspicious

You invested in some cryptocurrency a few years ago, and received two physical token coins to prove your investment. Usually they're stashed away in a safe location, but you've received information that one of the tokens is a fake. You take them out to have a look.

Looks like whoever tipped you off is reliable – the coins are definitely not identical. **Apart from their rotation, can you find eight visual differences between the two coins?**

82. Minesweeping

Oh dear. You're just firing up your computer for a day's activity when you see a message flash up where your home screen ought to be:

Welcome, unlucky victim! I've taken over your system for a little while, to send you a message:

STOP INVESTIGATING ME. LEAVE ME ALONE.

I thought I'd send you a playful little warning in the form of a game. Remember that old-school game, Minesweeper? I've brought it back, just for you. Yay!

There are mines in some of the squares in the grid, and your job is to find them all. But unlike the guessing game of old, I've given you a few clues to let you find them all, because I'm just so good-hearted. Clues in squares reveal the number of mines in touching squares – including diagonally. No more than one mine may be placed per square, and there are no mines in the numbered squares.

Mark out where you think the mines are and, when you're finished, I'll let you know if you were right. If you're wrong, it's no big deal – I'll just wipe everything clean across your entire system. Bit of fun, really.

You'd better get cracking, then, hadn't you?

You don't like the look of this at all. You're stuck between a rock and a hard place, though – you can play the game successfully and find all the mines, but you just don't know if this person is playing fair. What if they are toying with you and will erase your systems anyway?

You see that there's a timer ticking over in the corner – it's not a countdown, but you don't know what they're timing you for. For better or worse, you decide you'll try and find all the mines – play them at their own game, literally – and deal with the consequences when they arrive.

Can you work out where all of the mines are hidden below, before this unknown assailant wages war on your software?

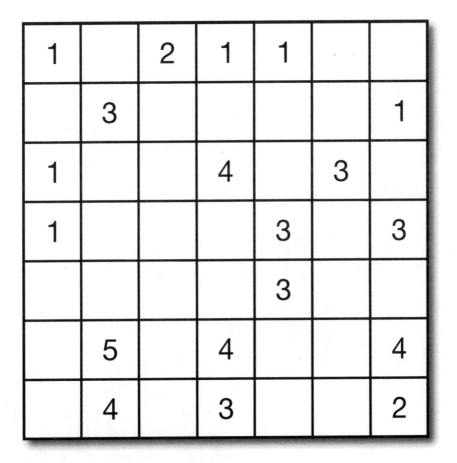

83. All Bar One

You've ordered some new hardware for your home system, after a few of your screens went on the blink. You usually have four screens in front of you, but you wanted a couple of spares so six boxes show up to your house.

You've never heard of anyone hacking into a screen itself before, but nevertheless something just doesn't seem right about this delivery. Perhaps you're a naturally suspicious person, but something's off. Has someone switched out one of the boxes?

Before you get bogged down in figuring out why someone would send you a dodgy screen, you decide to check the products over for yourself. Everything looks as it should, until you get to the barcodes on the base of each box. The products are identical, and therefore the barcodes should be too. But something's not right.

One of these barcodes is not like the others. **Which is the odd one out?**

C

9 734582122280-08

D

9 734582122280-08

E

9 734582122280-08

F

9 734582122280-08

125

84. Truck Track

You can't always fix every computer issue yourself, so sometimes even you have to call in the professionals. You've been tracking a shipment of hardware that should have been returned straight back to you after you sent it off for repair – but by the look of things it's been going around the houses. Literally. In fact, each of the dots below is a signal given off by the tracker you have fitted, marking a different stop on the journey from your house to the repair facility and back.

Can you join all of the dots to form a single loop, mapping out the journey your kit has taken? The loop does not cross or touch itself at any point. Only horizontal and vertical lines between dots are allowed, and some of the journey has already been filled in.

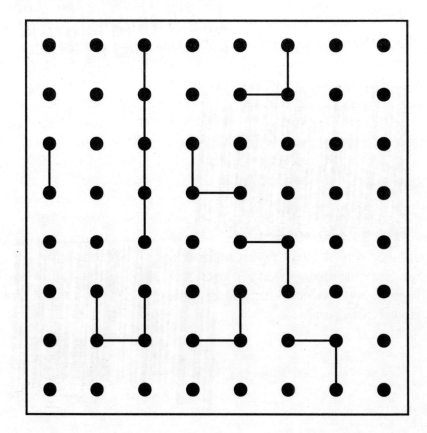

85. Quit Bugging Me

How annoying. Something on your machine is causing issues with certain files, creating anomalies in the metadata that defines the status of each document.

In one particular folder, each of your files can be individually locked and unlocked (by you and only you). Somehow, however, this bug is evidently able to lock and unlock files as it pleases. You can see it happening while you stare at the screen, perplexed, watching your files lock and unlock, seemingly at random.

But how random is it? You've been watching the folder for a while now, and usually all of the 100 files in the folder are kept locked for safety. They are named very simply, from just '1' to '100' to keep their contents inconspicuous.

At first, the bug went through every file in order, unlocking them one by one, starting with the first ('1'). Then, it went through toggling the lock status of every second file – i.e. starting with the '2' file, then '4' and '6' and so on, meaning these became locked again. Then, on the next round, it toggled the status of every third file, i.e. '3', '6' and so on – meaning that it locked the third file but unlocked the sixth, after it had just been locked in the previous round.

You realize that, if the bug carries on in this fashion, that perhaps after its 100th round of locking or unlocking it will have run out of files to start at, and hopefully stop. If, until then, it continues working in the same way for the 4th up to 100th rounds, **which files will be unlocked at the end of the bug's 100th run?**

127

86. Make It Count

You've been trying to access a network which dabbles in the dark web, but it's run by a deeply secretive organization. Not for the first time, you've come up against a wall of challenges designed to figure out if you're a bot – or worse, a cop. What's the benefit of being a computer genius if you still get held up in virtual traffic jams?

Some of the challenges are easier than others, especially when they come down to identifying a couple of easy pictures or the occasional famous face. There are the usual passcode hoops to jump through, although with enough AI skills you could probably find a way to bypass these pages altogether.

During one afternoon of surfing, however, you come across two images which look pretty unassuming:

A

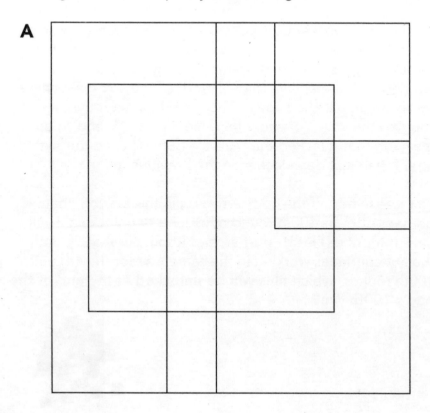

B

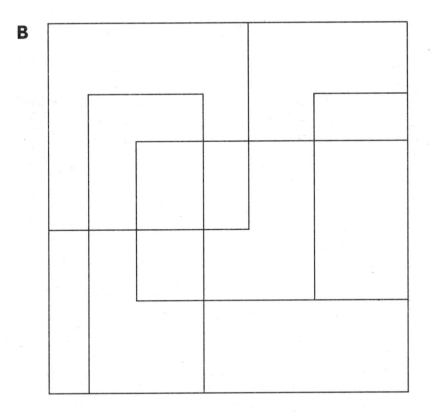

There's a message beneath the pair of images, with an apparently simple request:

COUNT THE NUMBER OF RECTANGLES IN EACH IMAGE – AND YES, A SQUARE COUNTS AS A RECTANGLE. WHICH IMAGE HAS MORE IN TOTAL? ANSWER A OR B TO CONTINUE, THEN PROVIDE THE TOTALS FOR BOTH IMAGES SO I CAN VERIFY IT WASN'T A LUCKY GUESS.

Seems like a pretty simple request, but when you get down to counting up the quadrilaterals you find there's more than first meets the eye. Counting everything from the big square around the outside of each image inwards, **what answers should you submit to the request?**

87. Without a Trace

Your apartment was broken into a while back, and you've just realized that they must have taken a USB stick which you suddenly need. You had a tracking device embedded in the stick, but they must have found it since it's clearly been disabled. Looks like you're not dealing with an amateur here.

A week or so later, an email pings into your inbox:

> Sorry about the breaking and entering fiasco but trust me, I really needed that USB stick. I'm not who you think I am, if you're thinking I'm a villain. I promise I haven't stolen anything else from you - real or virtual - but I just needed a copy of what was on that stick. Don't ask me how I figured out how to get to it.
>
> As a gesture of goodwill, I'm giving you the stick back. All the files are still on it, and nothing nasty (I swear) - I simply took a copy of the files for my own personal use. The stick is in a safety deposit box in a store two blocks away from you; there's a map to it attached to this email. Check your mailbox for the 4-digit code you'll need to open it.

You refresh your email inbox, but there's nothing else from this mystery sender. You check other email addresses you have, but there's nothing from them in any of those mailboxes either.

Finally, you check your real-life mailbox – the one attached to your front door – and see that there are two enigmatic pieces of paper in there. They've been at your property again!

The papers are translucent, like tracing paper. Both pieces have bars on them, but it's not obvious which way is up for each piece of paper – or even which side is the front or back.

Here's one piece:

And here's the other:

Why have they sent you this? **Can you figure out the 4-digit code you'll need for the safety deposit box?**

88. Shady Signal

Some days it just seems like everyone is out to get you, and today is no exception. You open up a page on your web browser to find that everything is blocked. Instead, no matter what you search for, you just see the following digit-filled grid:

2	6	8	6	0	4	0	6	4	0	0	4	2	0	4	8
0	4	2	0	4	0	0	1	3	8	2	4	0	6	2	0
0	0	6	0	2	0	7	9	5	3	0	0	2	8	0	8
0	6	8	0	6	3	5	4	8	1	7	2	0	0	2	4
2	0	0	2	0	1	2	8	0	4	3	0	6	8	6	0
4	0	2	0	4	1	6	1	3	0	9	4	0	2	0	6
6	4	6	0	5	7	0	9	5	6	1	7	6	0	0	4
2	8	0	8	9	0	6	3	9	0	4	9	4	0	4	0
0	2	6	3	1	2	0	1	3	8	0	1	9	6	0	0
0	0	0	1	6	4	0	5	7	0	4	6	5	0	2	4
4	0	5	9	0	4	6	0	4	8	2	0	3	1	0	0
8	8	7	8	0	8	0	3	7	4	8	2	8	1	0	2
6	1	1	2	6	2	8	9	5	0	0	0	6	3	7	6
0	9	6	8	0	4	0	0	0	2	0	4	8	8	1	4
2	7	3	1	9	1	7	5	5	3	1	9	3	1	5	0
0	6	0	0	4	0	6	0	4	0	0	4	2	0	0	2

Not very helpful, especially when you have projects to be getting on with. What's behind this?

You realize that if you hover over certain numbered squares with your mouse, they become shaded – at least until you move your mouse away. You don't want to click on any of the numbers in case you're taken somewhere on the net that you really don't want to be, but you're intrigued.

Suddenly a message pops up below the number grid:

Hi there. Wondering what's going on? I would be too.

As you can see, it's all too easy for me to get to you - virtually, that is. You've been snooping around a little too much for my liking, so I thought I'd stop by and make myself known. Consider this a friendly warning: stay away from my servers and I'll stay away from you.

Hope you're enjoying the numbers game. I drew you a pretty picture to remind you of my feelings. You can take a sneak peek for yourself: just remember to make sure that anything odd stays in the shadows.

Understood?

Ciao for now...

The message stays on your screen, and so do the numbers. As you wave your mouse around, you wonder why some of the numbers shade in while the pointer is over them while others don't.

You decide to try and uncover this so-called picture they've left behind for you – and then realize there's a clue in their third paragraph.

Can you reveal the hidden image within the number grid?

89. Drop-Off Point

You've been looking into some suspicious activity at a big business, and after taking a snoop through their databases you've found so many strange things that you feel confident that there's corruption to be uncovered. In particular, you think you might be able to find the tracking details to intercept a highly dubious-sounding shipment that they're planning to deliver in the next few months. You could alert the authorities – or keep the spoils for yourself – but either way, there's still a bit of detective work to be done.

The name of the country and city where the drop will take place, as well as the month and weekday of the drop, have been partially decoded below. Each word is still in fragments, so **can you match up the partial words to establish the exact details of the drop?**

AGU	ASU	AY	DAY
DN	ER	ES	MB
NCI	ON	PAR	PTE
	SE	WE	

Write the details in the gaps below, once you have them:

Country: _____

City: _____

Month: _____

Weekday: _____

90. Search and Rescue

A client has asked you to access and decode some encrypted files, then comb through them for certain information. It's a huge amount of data, and you need to open each file by hand due to the nature of the content you're searching for.

They're on a tight turnaround, so you only have 24 hours to complete the task from when you start looking through the files. Luckily, they're paying you a fortune.

You start checking through for the content you need, making notes as you go. There are 8,448 files to check – OMG – but you've started at a rate which means you should get them all done exactly on time. You know you can keep the rate constant, so you mentally switch off a little and try to get yourself 'into the zone'.

After a while, however, you realize that you don't seem to be finding anything useful, and time feels like it's dragging. Confused, you then realize that the clock you've been using actually isn't accurate at all, and you're not working at the rate you thought you were. In fact, it's taken you three times as long as you thought it would to look through the first 2,816 files. Uh oh!

You realize you'll need to calculate a new number of files you'll now need to check per hour to complete the task on time. **What was your previous actual hourly rate, and how long do you now have remaining to get the job finished?**

91. Magic Square

You're trying to enter an encrypted chatroom, and there's one final hoop to jump through. You've been circling the group for a while, and you hope your patience will be worth the wait: the members inside the forum have the potential to be very useful allies in the future. In this world, it helps to have a few friends you can trust. The group has already made contact – and you have successfully worked out a 4-digit passcode to give them – but it seems they're still not satisfied, as you haven't heard anything back. Annoying.

You check your email inbox, and in your junk folder is a message that's been sitting there a few days. Oh. It looks very much like it's from one of the chatroom members you were hoping to get involved with. Here's what they said:

You're almost there. If it was just me I'd let you in right now, but the rest of the group have prepared one more challenge so they can be sure. We've had so many problems in the past that I can't blame them. Let's consider it a final rite of passage.

Attached to this email is an image. You'll notice there are some empty spaces. You need to fill them with the digits 1 to 9, using each digit exactly once each. When all the numbers are placed, read the digits in the shaded squares from top to bottom to retrieve a 4-digit code to use in your reply to this email.

Oh, and you can't just place the numbers randomly. Make sure everything adds up equally.

Once you've sent us the code, you're in - provided it's correct, of course. Good luck!

Well that all sounds pretty straightforward. You open the email attachment they sent you and, sure enough, it's a grid with some empty squares:

11	24		20	
	12	25		16
17		13	21	
10	18		14	22
23		19		15

But how are you supposed to know where to put the numbers? You check back to the message, and see they've underlined something they must think is pretty crucial.

It seems you must make each row and column add up to the same total value. Given this, where should the digits be placed and **what is the 4-digit code?**

92. Behind the Mask

Something very weird is going on. You're part of an online community forum where hackers and computer geeks can talk, swap ideas and discuss all things tech – completely anonymously.

Members who join are assigned a username, which is a random combination of upper-case letters and numbers. The community is usually surprisingly respectful and calm, although you've noticed things can get a little heated in the smaller chatrooms that function like breakout zones, usually stemming from disagreements over bigger discussions.

A couple of weeks ago you must have upset somebody big-time, because when you post to the forum you notice that your username has been corrupted. Everyone else's usernames are appearing as normal, but yours looks like a mess of overlaid symbols. You try to post again, and your username looks different this time – but still corrupted. After your fourth attempt, someone sends you a private message via the community chat:

Hi there 'friend'. Notice anything unusual about your username today?

Let us introduce ourselves. We are a team of four professionals who operate on the side of the law that best suits us. We know you're familiar with our work, so we're here with a simple message:

Stop discussing our work on this chatroom. Stop trying to unmask us. You've seen what we can do to this secure forum. Just imagine what we could do to your servers, which we notice are considerably less well protected.

Seriously, though, just leave us alone. It'll be better for everyone if you do.

Not very friendly. Of course, you have no intention of stopping your investigations but you can at least try a bit harder to make sure they don't find out. You'd better check your server logs, too.

When you look more closely at your username, you realize that the four different corrupted versions do all still contain your five random characters, as well as five others. In fact they don't seem to have changed your username at all but have merely installed a hack to overprint it with other symbols – and it could even be that they are simply overprinting with their own usernames.

BZ9036

8174026

XTF345

XR410 35

What are the four usernames that are overprinting your own, and are quite possibly those of the people who are threatening you?

93. Sequence of Events

You've just bought some software that you're hoping will give you a better chance at detecting network incursions. You've made yourself into a bit of a target over the last few months; it seems like you barely go a day without encountering a threat of some kind. Luckily, you seem to have dodged the worst of the attacks. You're just about to install the software when a message pops up:

ENTER 4-DIGIT CODE PROVIDED

Unfortunately, you don't know what it's talking about. What four-digit code? Provided where?

The software was bought from a real store, and came in a box with a user's booklet in it. So far, so old-school. You flick through the book and you can't find anything about a code anywhere – although it does mention there will be some security steps to take before you can install the software.

You reach the back page of the manual, and there's just some more blurb about how great the software is. Not that great if you can't get into it! At the bottom, however, you notice that the page has some numbers stamped onto it, like this:

1. 14 25 36 X7 58 69 70 81

2. 124 115 10X 100 94 89 85 82

3. 14 28 42 56 7X 84 98 112

4. 15 2X 39 51 63 75 87 99

Hmmm. You need a four-digit code, and there are four lines of numbers here. There are also four digits apparently missing...

What is the four-digit code that you require to continue?

94. Mind Games

You're trying to uncover a list of passwords commonly used by a particular target online. You know they're a scientist who has previously used the names of chemical elements to create passwords because, ridiculously enough, they emailed the list of elements to themselves so they wouldn't forget!

When you open the email, however, the text looks corrupted – all the element names are jumbled up. **Can you figure out which ten chemical elements they've listed**, these being the ones they are most likely to use in their passwords?

×

NONE

BANCOR

IMZORUNIC

EDGYHORN

TOBLAC

KLECIN

NICSOIL

GENUSMAIM

UTOPIASMS

HUBSMIT

95. See Here

For obvious reasons, you like to keep pretty tight security around your home. There's a camera outside your front door, mainly so you can keep an eye on anyone who comes knocking. You've never had any trouble before – after all, barely anyone really knows where you live – so you're surprised one day to see that the feed was cut for several minutes. That's odd.

When you get back to your house to have a look, you're pretty sure something's not right. In fact, it looks a lot like someone has tampered with your security system.

The image on the left is the main security panel as you left it this morning, and the one beneath is what you came home to. Something has definitely changed.

Can you spot the five differences between the two panels?

96. The Arrangement

You've been snooping around on an underground gaming forum recently, keeping an eye on a few specific users. You think they might be sending malicious spyware to the other members in the forum, but you need to get closer to the suspects before you can find out more.

After a deep dive into one of the suspect's accounts, you come up against a security wall – obviously your repetitive activities are starting to make you look like a bot. You'll need to pass a visual test before you can carry on with your search.

Mentally rearrange the squares below so that none of the partial '4's are cropped off. **How many '4's appear in total?**

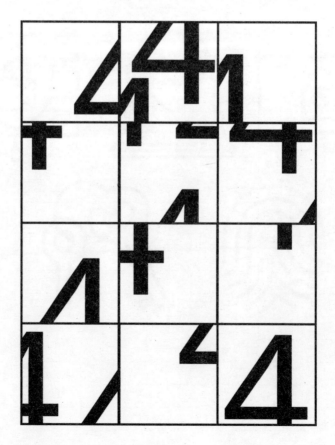

97. Friend or Foe

You've made contact with a couple of gamers who you think might be ethical hackers. After introducing yourself – and making an offer to work together on some good-cause hacking – you get the following reply:

Game on! We like that you've put your trust in us, but how do you know if we're the good guys or not? Here's a little test for you while you decide whether you'd like to buddy up with us.

Everything we make as a pair, we split between us. If you join us and we make profit, we'll split it three ways. So shade out anything that can't be split exactly three ways below. What are you left with?

1	7	2	7	2	12	6	3	3	9	3	5	1	2	7	2
5	8	8	1	3	9	11	5	7	1	9	3	8	11	5	4
11	1	2	6	9	13	11	1	4	14	7	12	6	1	1	2
14	8	9	3	4	14	4	8	2	11	1	4	9	15	14	8
4	3	6	2	14	7	2	4	5	1	8	14	8	6	12	1
3	3	8	1	12	6	9	1	13	6	3	9	1	1	9	6
9	1	4	5	3	14	3	1	8	12	13	9	5	14	2	9
3	4	14	8	6	12	9	8	1	3	12	6	7	11	13	3
12	7	1	5	4	4	5	1	4	7	2	14	5	4	7	6
9	13	4	5	9	8	1	2	1	1	2	6	1	8	14	3
15	3	14	13	3	12	14	4	7	11	3	12	8	5	9	12
14	6	3	7	1	9	3	8	1	12	9	14	4	3	6	2
4	1	12	9	1	4	12	6	3	6	8	1	6	3	1	5
5	7	8	3	6	14	1	8	2	11	14	9	12	5	8	7
1	7	1	13	9	3	7	7	1	4	3	6	13	1	2	7
5	1	8	2	5	6	12	3	6	12	9	4	2	11	8	2

98. Getaway Car

You've been piecing together a load of CCTV footage to try and track down some stolen goods which have been dumped somewhere in the city. You think that, somewhere in the pile of loot, is a valuable data stick which was taken from you after a break-in. After some investigating, you suspect that the car being used to transport the goods stopped under a bridge for some time – perhaps to stash them in a hidden location.

On the aerial map below, there's only one route from the top to the bottom without retracing steps, although it does involve going under and over bridges. In fact, it goes both over *and* under a few of the bridges. You think the stick is under the third such double-used bridge. **So where is it?**

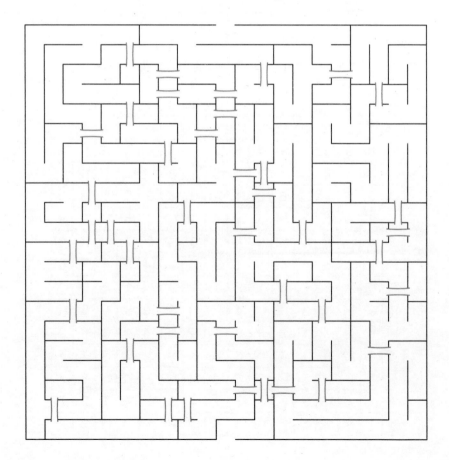

99. You're Missing Out

While looking through some classified files on behalf of a confidential client, you come across a folder where all of the file names consist purely of digits.

Your client is convinced that a file in this folder has been deleted without their knowledge – but they're struggling to work out which one, given that some of the file names are so similar in appearance.

You take a look at the list of names attached to each of the documents. Upon closer inspection, there's definitely a pattern to these numbers – and there's definitely a file missing, then. These are the names:

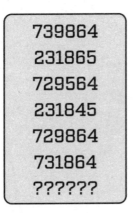

739864
231865
729564
231845
729864
731864
??????

From the options given below, **which option is the only number which could belong to the missing file?**

A. 721864

B. 731865

C. 231844

D. 721865

100. Remaking History

You've been working with a hacker that started stealing information from some high-profile people decades ago. So old-school is their operation, in fact, that they stored all of their incriminating evidence on floppy disks.

Your 'colleague' is in a predicament, however. Someone has shown up at their apartment and tried to smash up all of the evidence that might be lingering on the disks. Several of them, it seems, have been cut into two – and not neatly. Looks like the assailant was in a hurry to get the job done.

There's one particular disk that your hacker friend is keen to piece together. The top half of this disk matches with exactly one of the bottom halves shown on these pages. **Which one?**

A

B

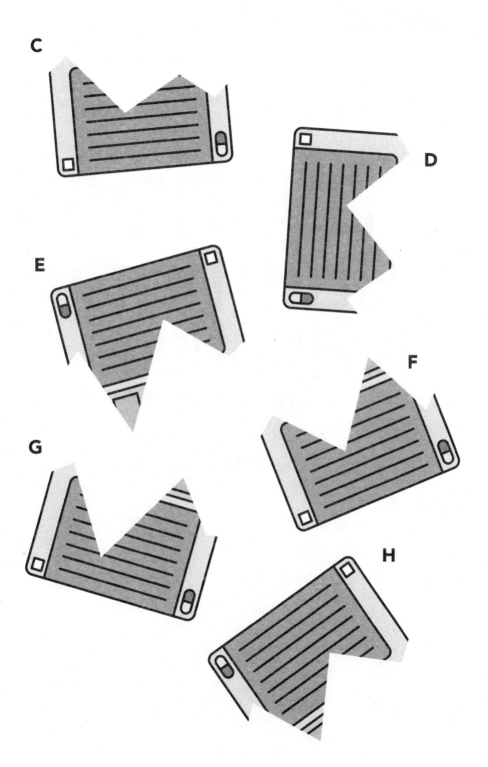

C

D

E

F

G

H

Solutions
Solutions
Solutions
Solutions

Solutions

1. Logging In
It is indeed your log-in PIN, which consists of the digits **2173**:

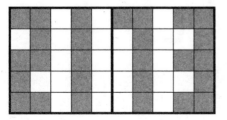

2. Odd and Even
BANKRUPTS. Each letter has a number from 1 to 9 above it, with odd and even numbers split between two different messages. Read all of the letters in order of their associated number, from 1 to 9, to reveal the password.

3. Binary Problem

1	0	0	1	0	0	1	1
1	0	0	1	0	1	1	0
0	1	1	0	1	0	0	1
1	0	0	1	0	1	1	0
0	1	1	0	1	1	0	0
0	0	1	0	1	0	1	1
1	1	0	1	0	1	0	0
0	1	1	0	1	0	0	1

The passcode is therefore **11010100**.

4. Funny Turn
The arrows at the bottom of the email are instructing you to rotate each of the figures in the various directions and amounts shown. If you obey the arrows, the following is revealed:

Solutions

311372

Your username is therefore **311372**.

5. The Counterfeit Chips

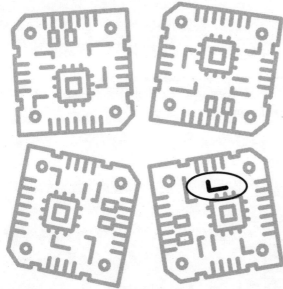

The odd chip out is **D**.

6. Corrupted Transmission

If you read the lines in plain English, the final two lines provide instructions as to what to do: 'I am your Omega. Pay attention to only my symbol'. Therefore you must only pay attention to the omega symbols, 'Ω'. Read only the letters directly above the omega symbols to reveal the following, adding spaces as appropriate: **'Open the attachment'**.

Solutions

7. The Strange Printout
The letters are stretched so that they are much taller than they would normally be printed. Reading them carefully reveals an instruction to 'Read the sixth letter of each separate line'. This then results, if you add a space at the appropriate position, in the following message (reading from top to bottom): '**HELP ME**'.

8. The Digital Clock
The '0's represent 'off' and the '1's represent 'on'. If you cross out the black segments that are marked as 'off', those that are left reveal the time **21:37**:

9. Secret Signals
Their number is +**4692857193**, and their name is **Chad**. They have replaced both their phone number and name with a simple letter-to-number exchange, where A=1, B=2, C=3 and so on.

10. Keep Your Friends Close
Marco is the engineer living in Sydney. Hopper is an accountant, and Jack is a police officer – although it's not possible to work out from the information given which one lives in which city.

11. Find the Pattern
The first three-digit number in each password is 111 lower than the equivalent in the previous password. For the subsequent three three-digit numbers within each password, a constant number is subtracted from the starting number at each step. For the first password, 9 is subtracted three

Solutions

times from 999, to give 990, 981 and 972. Together they form the password 999-990-981-972. Then, for each subsequent password, the amount subtracted at each step increases by 9. So, by the sixth password, which must start with 444, the value 54 will be subtracted at each step to give a sixth password of: **444-390-336-282**.

12. Building Blocks

Two of the digits in the 'revert' code, 7 and 1, are already given. Looking at the images, it can be observed that image 7 has the greatest number of cubes. If the number of cubes in each image is counted, it can similarly be observed that image 1 has the sixth-greatest number of cubes and therefore provides the sixth digit. When placed in descending order of number of cubes, the following image ordering – which is the required 'revert' code – results:
726381594.

13. Network Connect

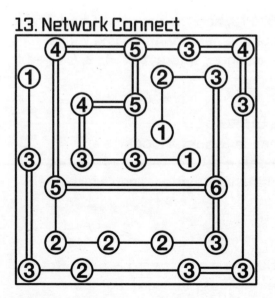

Solutions

14. Fight or Flight

Each of the four-digit numbers is a time, written in 24-hour clock format. The added or subtracted number on each line is a number of hours to change the first clock time to the second clock time result. The full set should therefore read:

- 11:43 + 15h = 02:43

- 18:05 + 4h = 22:05

- 01:23 – 4h = 21:23

- 08:08 – 8h = 00:08

- 11:11 + 11h = 22:11

- 14:22 – 3h = 11:22

- 23:45 + 1h = 00:45

The question-mark digits taken together are: **28225**.

15. The Search is On

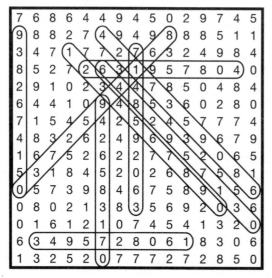

The code you need is **5160834972**.

Solutions

16. Dramatic Downloads
The true file sizes are as follows:

- 69MB
- 424MB
- 637MB
- 423MB
- 495MB

The total is therefore 2,048MB, or **2GB**.

17. Asterisky Business
Each of the asterisks has a different number of prongs, and the counts of these prongs represents a number. So, reading from left to right, the unlock code is therefore **5867**.

18. Isolation Issues

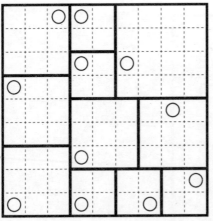

Solutions

19. Divide and Recover

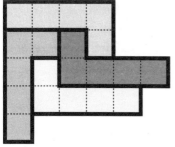

20. No Repeats

4	5	7	4	8	1	8	6	5	0
5	2	4	7	7	8	9	7	5	1
6	5	1	7	7	8	0	0	9	6
9	6	9	0	5	1	9	3	3	6
6	7	8	2	2	4	0	2	5	0
1	6	1	3	6	6	8	1	2	7
2	5	4	5	8	9	6	3	4	6
0	3	8	4	6	0	0	0	4	4
3	2	0	1	9	7	4	8	6	5
4	6	4	5	1	5	3	6	1	3

The code is **3201974865**.

21. Threat Levels

The image is a symbol indicating an **on/off switch**. The hacker friend is suggesting they could 'switch you off'.

Solutions

22. Unite and Conquer
Read one letter from Email 1, then one from Email 2, and so on reading left to right and top to bottom as normal. The letters reveal the message: **FIND MY SECRET ONLINE FOLDER**.

23. The Drop
The shadows behind each bold number reveal the original ordering of the digits:

The access code you need is therefore **56328**.

24. Scanned Entry
The barcode isn't a barcode at all, but a series of stretched digits which can be seen by bringing the bottom of the paper up to your eye level and looking along the length of the tall numbers. The following digits appear in the sequence:

7294659285205762004863846582756397583759331

Taking every fifth digit from this sequence gives the passcode: **65686559**.

25. Microdots
Overlay the two images one on top of one another to reveal the outlines of the four digits you require: **4, 9, 1 and 7**.

Solutions

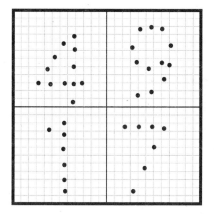

26. Enter at Risk

The routes through each building are as follows:

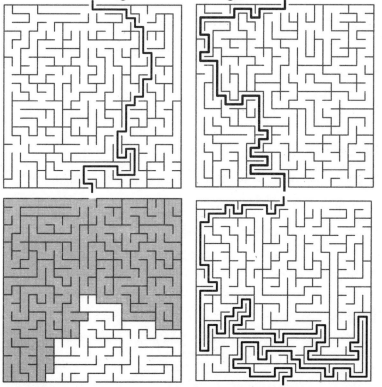

Building C is therefore the only one in which you can't exit through a different door to the one which you came in via.

Solutions

27. Image Issues

Rearrange the 12 image segments to reveal the following:

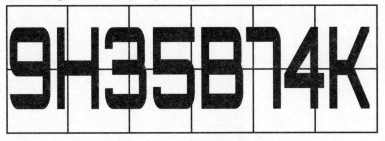

The username is therefore **9H35B74K**.

28. Crack the Code

Each of the four-digit numbers beneath an arrow symbol represents the exact appearance of that symbol as follows:

- 9 = long arrow pointing up
- 3 = no long arrow pointing up
- 4 = long arrow pointing down
- 7 = no long arrow pointing down
- 8 = short arrow pointing up
- 2 = no short arrow pointing up
- 6 = short arrow pointing down
- 1 = no short arrow pointing down

Therefore the prompt image corresponds to the following four-digit number: **3786**.

29. It All Adds Up

You have **6 devices** set up, requiring **12m** of red cabling.

Solutions

30. Missing Links

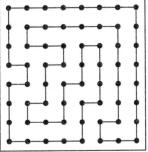

31. Fitting In

3	6	4	9
	1		
6		7	
2	5	3	1
8			3
7	9	6	5
	4		2
	2		
	8	7	1	4

The code that doesn't fit is therefore **5896**.

32. Through the Keyhole

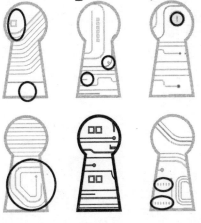

161

Solutions

33. Mixed Messages

Turn the 'binary' image clockwise by 90 degrees, until the top line matches the '4' in the guide your friend sent you. It should then look like this:

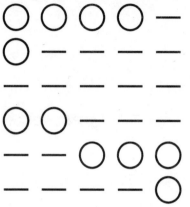

Then, read off the remaining numbers according to the guide to give the code: **410279**.

34. Spin Cycle

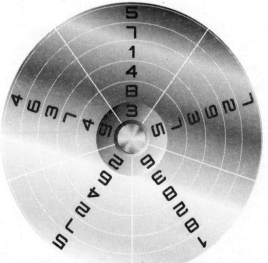

The access code is **384175**.

Solutions

35. Handy Coordination

3	6	2	5	4	1
1	5	4	3	2	6
4	2	5	6	1	3
6	3	1	2	5	4
5	1	3	4	6	2
2	4	6	1	3	5

The coordinates are therefore **31°46′52″N** and **15°43′26″E**.

36. QR Query

Codes **C** and **F** are identical.

Solutions

37. Decisions, Decisions

- Client F is offering you the most money, for 10 days' work.
- Client R is offering you the least money, for 15 days' work.
- Client Q is offering you 30 days' work.

38. Blocked Off

Imagine seeing the group of buildings from a top-down perspective:

The bird's-eye view shows a series of three digits, with the central digit distinguished by the lighter blocks: **074**.

39. Lead the Way

Starting at the letter 'x', trace a path by moving one square at a time following the directions of the arrows. The path created is the following:

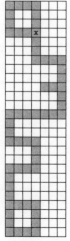

The four-digit passcode is therefore **9356**.

Solutions

40. Skimming Sequence

Ignoring the dashes in the long numbers, each long number is a simple sequence created by adding the first digit to itself repeatedly. For the first listed number, 6 is the first digit, and adding 6 to this gives the next two digits, 12, and then again to give the following two digits, 18, and so on. Dashes are added in after every fourth digit to given them the appearance of real card details. The most likely one of the four options is therefore the only one which fits this sequence rule, which is **option b: 2468-1012-1416-1820.**

41. Out of Space

If the 16 sticks in the overspill and the 14 potential new spots equal 60% of the original capacity, then 100% of the capacity in the original box must be 50. **So the current box can fit 50 USB sticks, and you have 66 sticks.**

42. Fingerprints

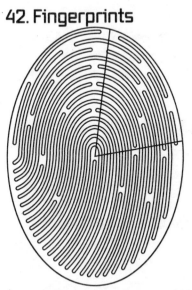

Only the top-left image fits exactly with the whole fingerprint.

Solutions

43. The Key

Imagine pressing the keys in the order indicated by the numbers. On a regular keyboard, they would type out the number to call: **639182754**.

44. Hiding Inside

Each outlined white digit is acting as a window onto another black-filled digit inside it:

The four-digit number is therefore **0785**.

45. Time is Missing

Imagine viewing the clock with a 'darker background' so that the black segments vanish and just the lighter ones remain. Reading only these lighter shaded segments reveals a remaining time of **05:48:31**.

46. Journey Jumble

Unscramble the letters in the names to reveal the following cities:

- LISBON

Solutions

- BUDAPEST
- OTTAWA
- HELSINKI
- CANBERRA
- SINGAPORE
- NAIROBI
- JAKARTA

47. Set the Bar

The first step is to work out what feature unites the four barcodes that were sent first. The secret is to read the thin and thick vertical bars from left to right (ignoring the extra-thick bars that start and end the entire barcode). The number of thick bars in each group follows an arithmetic sequence, as follows:

- Top-left barcode: 1 thick, 1 thin, 2 thick, 1 thin, 3 thick, 1 thin, 4 thick, 1 thin, 5 thick, 1 thin, 6 thick, 1 thin and then thick until the end of the barcode.

- Top-right barcode: 2 thick, 1 thin, 4 thick, 1 thin, 6 thick, 1 thin, 8 thick, 1 thin and then thick until the end of the barcode.

- Bottom-left barcode: 3 thick, 1 thin, 6 thick, 1 thin, 9 thick, 1 thin and then thick until the end of the barcode.

- Bottom-right barcode: 4 thick, 1 thin, 8 thick, 1 thin, 12 thick, 1 thin and then thick until the end of the barcode.

From the options they supplied you with, only the bottom-left option, labelled '3' has a similar pattern. In fact, it follows next in the sequence with a thin bar after five thick bars and then one after ten. So the answer is **barcode 3**.

Solutions

48. Go With the Flow

You need to find four digits, so start at the top of the chart by considering each of the nine possible digits in the range given (1 to 9) in turn and seeing if you can trace it to the bottom of the flow chart by answering the decision node. For example:

- 1 is not even so follow the 'x' to the right beneath the 'Even?' decision box. It is not prime, so follow the 'x' to the right beneath the 'Prime?' decision box. It is however a cube, so follow the tick to the left of of the 'Cube?' decision box. This means it ends up in the 3rd output box, reading left to right.

- 2 is even so follow the tick to the left beneath the 'Even?' decision box. It is also prime, so follow the tick to the left beneath the 'Prime?' decision box. This means it ends up in the 1st output box, reading left to right.

- 3 is not even so follow the 'x' to the right beneath the 'Even?' decision box. It is prime, so follow the tick to the left beneath the 'Prime?' decision box, and end up at the 'STOP' end point. So there is no '3' in the four-digit code.

- And so on for the remaining digits.

The four-digit code is therefore **2419**.

49. Key Problem

168

Solutions

50. Going Back in Time

The whole set of timestamps is being viewed as though reflected vertically. When flipped upright, the following times are shown – which are now in chronological order, as required:

01:08:26

12:53:19

17:39:00

22:05:46

51. Caught in the Web

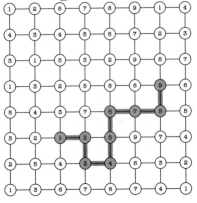

52. Dial It In

Imagine laying the two images so the one with holes is placed on top of the other, making sure that both remain facing 'up' as shown, and aligning the two pointers. The following numbers will appear in the holes, which can then be ordered

Solutions

from largest to smallest as instructed to give the solution of **987641**.

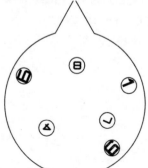

53. It's a Date

The alarm code is therefore **6320**.

54. Attachment Issues

The Green file is 4MB and the Blue file is 2MB. **Therefore only the Red file, which is 3MB, is safe to open.**

55. Missing Pieces

- CASE
- SCREEN
- MOUSE
- HARD DRIVE
- MONITOR

Solutions

- MOTHERBOARD
- KEYBOARD
- COOLING FAN

56. The Motherboard

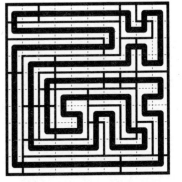

57. Addressing the Problem

7	8	1	6	4	2	3	5
5	2	4	3	6	8	7	1
3	6	5	1	2	4	8	7
2	4	7	8	3	5	1	6
1	3	8	5	7	6	2	4
6	7	2	4	1	3	5	8
8	1	6	2	5	7	4	3
4	5	3	7	8	1	6	2

The IP address to block is therefore: **72.58.73.42**.

58. Fickle Friend
The numbers, in the order specified, are:

- ONE
- THREE
- FIVE

Solutions

- SEVEN
- EIGHT
- NINE

The passcode is therefore **135789**.

59. Meet in the Middle

Say that the distance from your office to your friend's is represented by d. Then in total you have walked $2(1200 + (d - 1800)) = 2400 + 2d - 3600 = 2d - 1200$. Conversely your friend has walked $2((d - 1200) + 1800) = 2d - 2400 + 3600 = 2d + 1200$.

If you had met in the middle – equidistant from both offices – then you would each have walked exactly twice the distance d between the offices, since you would have walked halfway and back each of the two days. So $2d$ is equal to the distance you would each have walked had the total distances been the same for both of you. As worked out above, you have in fact walked 1,200m *less* than $2d$, and your friend has walked 1,200m *more* than $2d$. **Therefore your friend walked 2,400m further in total**.

60. Chain Mail

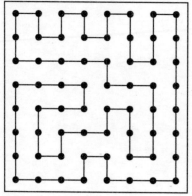

Solutions

61. Pixel Problem

Each of the three-digit numbers beneath an image represents the exact appearance of that configuration as follows:

- 3 = black square on top row
- 7 = grey square on top row
- 4 = no shaded square on top row
- 6 = black square on middle row
- 2 = grey square on middle row
- 5 = no shaded square on middle row
- 9 = black square on bottom row
- 1 = grey square on bottom row
- 8 = no shaded square on bottom row

Therefore the code is **458**.

62. More Missing Pieces

- SPEAKERS
- MEMORY CARD
- SCANNER
- JOYSTICK
- PRINTER
- TOUCHPAD
- WEBCAM
- MICROPHONE

Solutions

63. To Your Own Devices

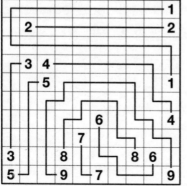

64. The Lighter Ones

Isolate the 'lighter ones' in the grid to reveal the following:

So the three digits in increasing value order are **3, 4 and 7.**

Solutions

65. It's Who You Know

66. Foreign Friends

- INDIA
- AUSTRALIA
- MOZAMBIQUE
- NORWAY
- VENEZUELA
- ESTONIA
- MONGOLIA
- ZIMBABWE

67. Crypto Contest

Ask your friend to put one real coin in one bag, and all the remaining coins in the other bag. Then, if the coin toss results in the bag with a single coin being chosen, you win. But you also have a chance of winning with the other bag, which has 3 out of 7 winning coins (a 3 in 7 chance) if chosen. Both bags are equally likely, so your overall chance of winning is $(1/2 \times 1) + (1/2 \times 3/7) = 1/2 + 3/14 = 10/14 = 5/7$. So you have a **5 in 7** chance of winning with this tactic – much better than 1 in 2.

Solutions

68. Ones and Zeros

```
1 1 0 1 0 0 0 0 0 1 1 0 1 0 1
1 0 0 0 0 1 1 0 1 1 0 0 0 0 1
0 1 1 0 1 0 1 0 0 0 1 0 1 0 0
0 0 0 0 1 0 0 0 0 1 1 0 0 0 1
0 1 1 0 0 0 1 0 0 1 0 0 0 0 1
1 0 0 1 0 1 1 0 0 0 0 1 0 0 0
1 0 0 1 0 0 0 1 0 1 0 1 0 0 0
0 0 1 0 0 0 1 0 1 0 0 1 0 1 1 0
0 0 1 0 1 0 1 1 0 0 0 0 1 0 1 0 0
0 0 0 0 1 0 0 0 1 0 0 0 0 1 0
1 0 1 0 0 1 0 1 1 0 0 1 0 1 0
0 1 1 0 0 1 0 0 0 1 0 1 0 0 1
0 1 0 1 1 0 1 1 0 1 0 0 1 0 1
0 0 1 0 0 1 0 0 0 0 0 1 1 0 0 0
1 0 1 0 0 1 0 0 1 0 0 1 0 1 1
```

69. Speed Search

The four-digit number is **8265**.

70. Pyramid Scheme

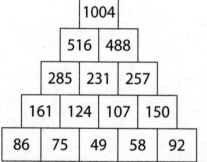

So the number at the top is **1004**.

Solutions

71. They've Got Mail

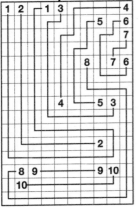

72. Networking Event

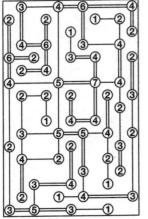

73. Number Plates

Your friend has sent back your list in a different order, with exactly one letter or number changed on each plate. From top to bottom on the second list, the changes are:

- M has changed to C

- 2 has changed to 5

- K has changed to L

Solutions

- S has changed to F
- S has changed to R
- B has changed to J
- 5 has changed to 2

There are seven plates, and seven possible positions for changes, given that each number plate has seven characters. There is only one change per character position across the plates; read them out in order from left to right to reveal the correct number plate of **CL25 JRF**.

74. Phone a Friend

7	4	2	1	3	5	9	6	8
6	5	1	8	9	7	4	2	3
8	3	9	2	6	4	1	7	5
1	9	5	7	4	3	2	8	6
2	8	4	6	5	1	7	3	9
3	6	7	9	8	2	5	1	4
5	2	8	4	7	6	3	9	1
4	1	6	3	2	9	8	5	7
9	7	3	5	1	8	6	4	2

Therefore the missing phone number is **759752352**.

75. Code-crack Hackers

Each of the three-letter codes in the larger image corresponds with a description of the square above it:

- F = black left bar
- Q = grey left bar
- R = grey right bar
- Z = white right bar
- M = black right bar
- J = star points up
- A = star points down

Therefore the three-letter code is **QZJ**.

Solutions

76. Around the Houses
The houses were snooped on in the following order:

1. Chicago

2. Malibu

3. Toronto

4. Cancun

5. Houston

6. Boston

7. Seattle

8. Miami

77. Back to Front
Their typed message is written backwards, and reads: TRY AGAIN – AND READ THE NUMBERS LIKE YOU WOULD READ THIS MESSAGE. The image your friend sent you has been mirrored around a vertical axis, meaning all of the dots and dashes representing the Morse code appear backwards. You must then interpret them using the table from '33. Mixed Message' on page 52. The code is therefore **83561**. The only correct digit was **5**.

78. Form of Address
Each of the IP addresses forms a sequence of four numbers which are progressively divided by a constant. In the first example, 216 divided by 6 is 36, and again is 6, and again is 1 – giving 216.36.6.1. All of the other IP addresses show similar geometric sequences. Therefore the only suggestion IP address option in the list which follows this pattern is **F: 1.1.1.1.**

Solutions

79. Blueprint Blues

Using basic geometry you can calculate the unlabelled areas on both maps for both units. Adding this up shows that Unit A has 96m² of floorspace, whereas Unit B has 97m². **Therefore the second floorplan, for Unit B, shows the largest overall area.**

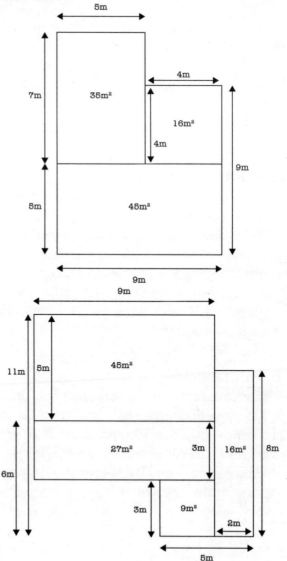

Solutions

80. Room for One More

The completed grid looks like this:

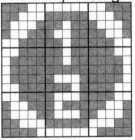

You therefore conclude that they are in **room 12**.

81. Bit Suspicious

82. Minesweeping

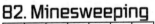

1	●	2	1	1		
	3	●			●	1
1		●	4	●	3	
1	●	●		3	●	3
		●		3	●	●
●	5	●	4		●	4
●	4	●	3	●	●	2

Solutions

83. All Bar One
Barcode D has bars which are shorter than the others on the very left-hand side. Could just be a printing glitch, but you can't be too careful...

84. Truck Track

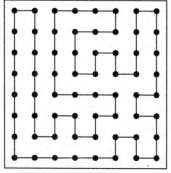

85. Quit Bugging Me
Any file which is a square number – **1, 4, 9, 16, 25, 36, 49, 64, 81** and **100** – will be unlocked, while the rest will be locked. This is because square numbers have an uneven number of factors – because one of the factors will be multiplied by itself to create the square – so they'll be in a different state to the locked state they began in before the first round.

Solutions

86. Make It Count
Image A has the most, with 25 rectangles/squares, while B has 22 rectangles/squares.

87. Without a Trace
Imagine that the two pieces of tracing-like paper are placed one on top of the other. If the first piece of paper is rotated 180 degrees and the bottom paper is turned over (and therefore mirrored left to right), the following image appears:

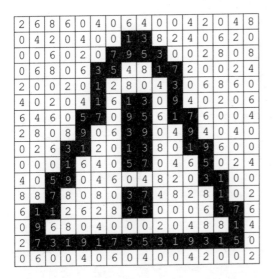

So the 4-digit code is **3724**.

88. Shady Signal
Shade in all squares containing an odd number (making sure that 'anything odd stays in the shadows') to reveal that the hidden image is a warning sign:

2	6	8	6	0	4	0	6	4	0	0	4	2	0	4	8
0	4	2	0	4	0	0	1	3	8	2	4	0	6	2	0
0	0	6	0	2	0	7	9	5	3	0	0	2	8	0	8
0	6	8	0	6	3	5	4	8	1	7	2	0	0	2	4
2	0	0	2	0	1	2	8	0	4	3	0	6	8	6	0
4	0	2	0	4	1	6	1	3	0	9	4	0	2	0	6
6	4	6	0	5	7	0	9	5	6	1	7	6	0	0	4
2	8	0	8	9	0	6	3	9	0	4	9	4	0	4	0
0	2	6	3	1	2	0	1	3	8	0	1	9	6	0	0
0	0	0	1	6	4	0	5	7	0	4	6	5	0	2	4
4	0	5	9	0	4	6	0	4	8	2	0	3	1	0	0
8	8	7	8	0	8	0	3	7	4	8	2	8	1	0	2
6	1	1	2	6	2	8	9	5	0	0	0	6	3	7	6
0	9	6	8	0	4	0	0	0	2	0	4	8	8	1	4
2	7	3	1	9	1	7	5	5	3	1	9	3	1	5	0
0	6	0	0	4	0	6	0	4	0	0	4	2	0	0	2

Solutions

89. Drop-Off Point
Country: PARAGUAY
City: ASUNCION
Month: SEPTEMBER
Weekday: WEDNESDAY

90. Search and Rescue
If you have checked 2,816 files then that's just a third of the full count of 8,448 files – but if it's taken you three times too long then you have used up the full 24 hours you assigned already. This means your effective rate has been 2816 ÷ 24 = **just over 117 per hour, and unfortunately you have no time at all remaining.**

91. Magic Square

11	24	7	20	3
4	12	25	8	16
17	5	13	21	9
10	18	1	14	22
23	6	19	2	15

The four-digit passcode is **7412**.

Solutions

92. Behind the Mask

Your username is X7425, so the other four are **BZ936, 8L3OG, VTP34 and YN163**:

X7425

BZ936

8L3OG

VTP34

YN163

93. Sequence of Events

Each row is a different number sequence, with one digit omitted from a number within that sequence and replaced by an 'X'. To identify the 'X's, work out what the sequences are:

1. Working from left to right, add 11 at each step – so the missing digit is the 4 in 47
2. Subtract 9, then 8, then 7, and so on – so the missing digit is the 7 in 107
3. Add 14 at each step – so the missing digit is the 0 in 70
4. Add 12 at each step – so the missing digit is the 7 in 27

Putting the results together creates the code **4707**.

94. Password Protected

- NEON
- CARBON
- ZIRCONIUM
- HYDROGEN

Solutions

- COBALT
- NICKEL
- SILICON
- MAGNESIUM
- POTASSIUM
- BISMUTH

95. See Here

96. The Arrangement

There are **six '4's** in the rearranged image.

Solutions

97. Friend or Foe

Shading in all of the numbers not divisible by 3 reveals a **smiley face** image, so it looks like they want to be friends, rather than foes. At least on the strength of this one image, anyway.

98. Getaway Car

Solutions

99. You're Missing Out

The files can be re-ordered in such a way that there is exactly one digit changed between each successive filename, were one extra file to be added in the location marked with '??????' below:

- 729564
- 729864
- 739864
- 731864
- ??????
- 231865
- 231845

The list could of course be written in the reverse order, but either way there's only one possible missing file name from the options given: **731865.**

100. Remaking History

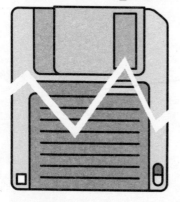

Option **F** is the correct bottom half.

Notes

Notes

Notes

Notes